Brief
History
of

SILVERTON

By Duane A. Smith

WESTERN REFLECTIONS
PUBLISHING COMPANY®

Montrose, Colorado

© 2004 Duane A. Smith
All rights reserved in whole or in part.

ISBN 1-890437-95-6

Library of Congress Control Number: 2003110250

Cover photo: Silverton and Sultan Mountain, Colorado; Detroit Photographic Co. (Courtesy P. David Smith)

Second Edition
Printed in the United States of America

Western Reflections Publishing Company®
219 Main Street
Montrose, CO 81401
www.westernreflectionspub.com

CHALLENGE OF THE SAN JUANS

This is a story about a town, its people, and its mines. Mining gave Silverton, Colorado its birth, and until the 1990s remained
its principal economic pillar. Today mining is often looked upon as
a pillager and raper of the environment; once it was honored for opening the West and developing the country. Damned and praised,
mining is not dead in the San Juans; someday it will reemerge. Meanwhile, we can see its heritage everywhere around Silverton.

To understand the story about to unfold, one must understand
the grasp that gold and silver had on those who sought these minerals. "Mining fever" we call it. A jovial Cleveland investor, who had
just lost $20,000 on a San Juan mine, said it best, "Well, I can't help
laughing when I think of what a d—d good thing we would have had
if we had only struck it."
Respected mining engineer and reporter, T.A. Rickard, gave the
industry's view, "There is as much luck in mining as in any other
business enterprise, hardly more; there is as much room for skill and
sense in mining as in other commercial undertakings, and a good
deal more."

Prospector/miner Nicholas Creede, who discovered silver just
over the mountains from Silverton, observed, "I never cared a great
deal for money, but had a great desire to find a great mine—something that would excite the world." He succeeded, but was not satis-
fied. "My desire to prospect is just as great, if not greater, than ever
before. It is not in my make up to sit down, cross my hands and do
nothing." Finally, an excited San Juaner wrote in the fall of 1874,
"The mines are a success, and in a few years this will be, not the
finest, but the richest and largest mining camp in the world."

Mining had another impact on the prospectors who searched,
the miners who dug, and the investors who risked capital. Wrote a
mining engineer, "It seems incredible that so few people connected
with mining are capable of telling the truth." The problem, as he saw

it, was "they either lie deliberately or they kid themselves or what is often worse, they are perfectly honest individuals who are unable to make reliable observations and draw conclusions there from." While he felt at the moment "it is a hell of a business," he continued mining. Once it gets in your blood, finding a cure is hard.

"Fever," wealth, fame, success, excitement—they lured miners from one mining rush to another for half the nineteenth century and into the twentieth. Men and women went where they might never have gone otherwise and put down roots. They needed something beyond the ordinary to face the challenge of the San Juans, the highest mining district and one of the most rugged in the United States. An early writer described the region in this fashion:

> It is the wildest and most inaccessible region in Colorado, if not in North America. It is as if the great spinal column of the continent had bent upon itself in some spasm of the earth, until the vertebra overlapped each other, the effect being unparalleled ruggedness, and sublimity more awful than beautiful. In the midst of a wild confusion of precipitous peaks and sharp ridges are a few small elevated valleys.

One of those "small elevated valleys" became home to Silverton.

Ringed by 12,000 and 13,000 foot peaks (the highest Sultan Mt. 13,368), Silverton sits in Baker's Park as it became known. At 9,300 feet in elevation, give or take a few feet depending where one is standing, this is a strikingly beautiful mountain valley. Mineral and Cement creeks join the Animas River in Baker's Park, providing an abundant water supply. The large valley also provided plenty of acreage to lay out a town in the traditional American grid pattern. None of this land could be called agricultural however. San Juan County is one of the few in the United States with no farm land.

The park sits on the southern edge of the Silverton caldera, a collapsed crater of an ancient volcano. There are several other calderas in what 27-28 million years ago was the San Juan volcanic field. Faulting and folding followed, along with glaciation, to shape the present valley. Along the faults, over time, acidic, mineral-laden water deposited metals such as gold, silver, lead, zinc, and copper. All would be found in and around Silverton.

4

These faults became the veins the miners so hoped to strike. The principal mines in the district are found on those faults, although to find them and work them successfully did not prove as easy it as it might sound. The veins consisted of a complex intermixing of various minerals, and finding the right reduction methods took time and money.

In the high optimism of the rush and development of the region, such factors little troubled men's minds. The important thing was to get there, find a mineralized outcropping, and stake a claim. The gold was there, the silver was there, just waiting to be mined by the fortunate individuals who found them. But wait! Martin Luther centuries before warned:

> Satan deludes many in mines, making them think they see great stores of copper and silver where there is none. If he can bewitch men in full daylight above ground, he can do so much more in a subterranean mine.

Bewitched or not, come and see a land that remained terra incognita to most Coloradans until well into the 1870s.

CHAPTER 1

EL DORADO

El Dorado! The Spanish sought it for centuries in the Americas. That elusive place fabled for its great wealth of gold and precious jewels, fired men's imaginations. It drove them daringly to explore, stubbornly colonize, and ruthlessly exploit. El Dorado was always somewhere that they were not—somewhere beyond the horizon.

Coronado came into the southwest in 1540 in search of the seven cities of Cibola, another variation of El Dorado. Spanish settlement was in the Rio Grande Valley by the 1590s and, despite a temporarily successful 1680 pueblo revolt, stayed there. New Mexico did not prove as mineral-rich as old Mexico. So the Spanish looked elsewhere for El Dorado. Eventually, they explored northward and reached a mountainous region they named the San Juans.

Certainly, by the time the English colonists were declaring their independence in 1776, the San Juan area was well known to the New Mexicans. That year, Domiguez and Escalante, two Spanish priests, led an expedition to try to find a route to the new Spanish settlements in California and along the way preach to the people they found. In their journal they reported when passing near the La Plata (Silver) mountains: "They say there are veins and outcroppings of metal.... The opinion formed previously by some persons from the accounts of various Indians and some citizens of this kingdom that they were silver mines caused the mountain to be called Sierra de la Plata."

The journal listed the geographic names of the region with the assurance that their readers knew what they were discussing. San Juans, La Platas, Animas, Mancos, Mesa Verde, and other names clearly showed that the Spanish had been active there for years. They did not, however, leave records to prove it. A fifth of all that was discovered or found, the royal fifth, was to be given to the king. The king and his court lived too far away, a year's travel nearly, so his New Mexico subjects prospected and mined a little in and around the

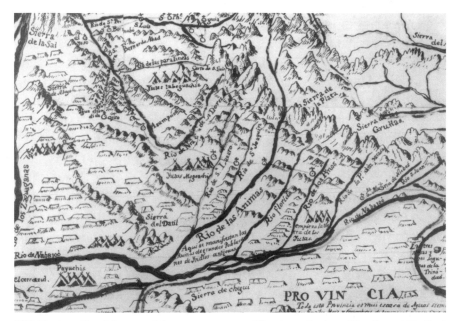

18th Century Spanish map of the area   (Courtesy: Center of Southwest Studies)

San Juans, but did not trouble his officials by telling them of their activities. Even some of his officials in Santa Fe were probably involved in these expeditions.

The Spanish came and they departed. They left behind geographic names, legends of lost mines and buried treasure, of treasure trains attacked, and the never to die belief that the San Juans were the mother lode of minerals. That they were in the San Juans, and undoubtedly in the Silverton area, cannot be questioned. The 1870s miners who came later uncovered European tools, mine portals, and other evidence that miners had dug there before them. In 1877, for example, near Lake Como, an "abandoned opened cut on a silver vein" was found. Traces of "drilling" and "tools" were also discovered, leading to speculation in local newspapers about who had been there and when.

The residents of the region looked with wonder on these European/American newcomers and their strange quest. The Utes, who called this land theirs for several centuries before the Spanish arrived, did not mine for precious or base metals.

Long before the Utes had ventured into the region, hunters and gatherers had wandered in seeking shelter and game. They evolved into the prehistoric pueblo people (Anasazi), who developed an advanced culture in the region, the best known locations of them being at Mesa Verde and Chaco Canyon. While they must have walked into the mountains to hunt or just to venture about, and perhaps pick up a pretty rock or two, they did not mine.

They were gone and their villages deserted by the end of the thirteenth century. Even the Utes had little memory of them. The Utes had no interest in El Dorado either, or the metals that the Spanish so treasured. The Utes, in fact, had alternated fighting and trading with these people coming from the south. In the end, they borrowed much from their culture, including that creature that changed their life forever, the horse. Other European wonders came also— iron pots, guns, knives, beads, mirrors. The Utes jumped from the stone age to the iron age.

The Utes hunted and lived in the San Juans during the summer but understandably chose to winter elsewhere. Once the Spanish arrived, they would never again have this land solely as their own. The Spanish left, then the newly independent New Mexicans came to trade and poke around. Soon fur trappers entered the region to tap a different natural resource—the beaver. They trapped in what passed for the San Juan spring and early summer, then came back during the longer fall, before heading to winter camp in lower, more sheltered valleys.

It might have seemed romantic and adventuresome. In reality, it proved hard, dangerous, and often low paying for the trappers in the field. Clerks in St. Louis and merchants in St. Petersburg charted the course of developments. For the first, but not the last time, the San Juans became part of a world wide economy and an economic colony for outside investors.

The fur trappers were not looking for gold or silver, but, undoubtedly, they knew it could be found in these mountains and elsewhere in the Rocky Mountains. They probably even prospected a little and no doubt turned up "color," although the San Juan mountains would never be famous for their free gold deposits.

Eventually the fur trade died, the victim of changing fashions and outside control. The first wave of exploitation had ended with the beaver almost exterminated. For a short time, the Utes again had the San Juans to themselves. Unknown to them, the outcome of the Mexican War transferred the region to the United States. Soon Indian agents appeared and the Utes signed treaties defining their land. The San Juans would be part of their reservation, guaranteed by the United States government. Unfortunately for the Utes, just as the Mexican War drew to a close, a chance discovery of gold in far off California in 1848 changed their life and history forever.

The 1849 gold rush changed America forever and influenced the world economy. People rushed to the mother lode country to make their fortune; most did not, but a legend was born. Mining, mining camps, wealth, rushes, excitement—Americans had never seen their like before. The Utes could not dream what was going to happen to their homeland and to them.

CHAPTER 2

HUMBUG!

The golden events that finally brought excited prospectors and miners into the San Juans happened in 1848-49 and 1858-59—the famous California and Pike's Peak gold rushes. The discovery of gold at Sutter's Mill on the south fork of the American River in January 1848 set off a chain reaction that for the next seventy years swept around the world. Gold, then silver and other minerals, were discovered in amounts totally unknown previously in world history.

At last, the dream of "getting rich without working" appeared to be a fact. Delighted and inexperienced people might have thought that mining proved that axiom, but an old-timer knew better: "I have never worked so hard in my life to get rich without working." That attitude told much about mining and the public's conception of the industry.

If there was one in California, it seemed logical that others must also exist. Off went the prospectors, scurrying up nameless creeks, then climbing over the next mountain into another enticing valley searching for El Dorado. Stay at home folks hoped they would find one nearer to them than time-consuming months away by slow wagon, or a costly sea voyage to California. Their wish came true.

"THE NEW EL DORADO!!! GOLD IN KANSAS TERRITORY!!"
"GOLD MORE PLENTIFUL THERE THAN IN CALIFORNIA   GOLD
FOUND ALL PLACES PROSPECTED"

The Pike's Peak country, only a thirty-day journey by wagon from the Missouri River, seemed the answer to their dreams.

In that wonderful spring of 1859, as war clouds gathered on the eastern horizon, somewhere around 100,000 people rushed westward—not to Pike's Peak, the only generally known geographic point, but to future Gilpin and Clear Creek counties. They soon claimed the best available sites, and prospectors scurried hither and yon, searching, always searching, for a golden bonanza. By fall they had crossed the "Snowy Range" and were in the future Breckenridge area.

The first prospectors into the San Juans in the 1870s confronted an uncharted mountainous region (Courtesy: U.S. Geological Survey)

They cursed the snow (it was not a money maker for them) and isolation, but sensed that even farther west might be other undiscovered mining regions.

In the transitory life of the prospector, something better always beckoned him on to search for the new El Dorado. Charles Baker was one of those individuals. In August he led a small party into what became known as Baker's Park. Nothing in Colorado was more isolated or more difficult to reach than the San Juans, yet Baker and his followers reached the very heart of the mountains. What brought them besides Spanish legends and fur trappers' tales will never be known. They found gold but did not try to keep their secret.

By that mysterious, always buzzing mining camp grapevine, hints of a bonanza spread. Increasingly favorable reports, however, gave only vague notions of location. In Denver, Cañon City, Santa Fe and the old village of Abiquiu, the story spread, and people made ready to rush to the new discoveries, "another California," when weather permitted in 1861.

11

Denver and Cañon City both claimed to be the gateway for people going to the "San Wan." A touch of skepticism and a stronger urban jealousy, when Cañon City seemed to be getting the better of the publicity, caused Denver's William Byers, owner and editor of the Rocky Mountain News, to cast a jaundiced eye on the proceedings. On November 9, 1860, he wrote that "very many of our people are becoming excited on the reported richness and promise of the San Juan mines." He did not stop there; "nothing has reached us of sufficient weight to warrant the rush to that mythical *dorado*." To him, all this excitement panned out to nothing more than "humbug."

A prospector, who signed his name G. W., wrote to the News after his return in late 1860 from the San Juans, "If this is a humbug—and there is but little doubt about that—it is a severe one, and disastrous to many." Even when concurring with Byers, he optimistically looked to 1861 when "the country would be thoroughly prospected." First hand knowledge did not dim future prospects for those afflicted with gold fever!

Humbug, nothing, indeed! Nevertheless, that did not stop interest, and even Byers started to hedge, while letters from Baker, praising his new district, arrived almost providentially. Enthusiastically, Baker predicted that 25,000 Americans would be in the region the next year to mine and farm.

Byers never completely capitulated. While telling readers that Denver was the place from which to start to the San Juans, he warned them about other stampedes in California that ended with the disillusioned and disappointed stampeders rushing back "home to the states."

That did not stop folks from trudging off for the San Juans through near desert land and high mountains. The maybe 800-1,000 who reached Baker's Park, over Baker's toll road and past Baker's camp, called Animas City, mined disappointment and hard times, not gold. Byers had been more correct than maybe even he wanted to be. Little gold was found, the Utes were not pleased with this invasion of their land, and the isolation and weather affected everybody. All this on top of the time, struggle, and expense of reaching

Bakers Park from the mouth of Arrastra Gulch, photo taken by William H. Jackson in 1874
(Courtesy: U.S. Geological Survey)

the so-called "better than California" site killed interest in staying.

"An old experienced miner" said the country, "did not look right for gold." When the best pan produced only $2.50 in gold, most only a few flakes, these pioneering San Juaners had suffered too long on hope. That proved enough and they raced out, "the worse used up and most ragged men that I ever saw" one remembered.

Out they came, sadder, though perhaps not wiser. One group, running out of food before reaching "civilization" boiled their moccasins to make a "soup" to survive. Some diehards lingered in Baker's Park all summer; eventually they left, too, and everything was abandoned—the park, Animas City, and the dreams of those who had staked so much on the San Juans. It would be long after the guns of the Civil War fell silent that again the silence of the San Juans would be broken by mining.

These early San Juaners failed because there had not been enough gold. The isolation and elevation further dampened their enthusiasm. Shortages of supplies and actual starvation faced those who braved the inhospitable San Juans and their changeable weather. Troops, too, were withdrawn to march back east to fight in the Civil War. Needed government protection and involvement were simply not to be found in the next few years. More important matters occupied Abraham Lincoln's administration.

The miners left behind scars on the land, broken sluice boxes, deserted cabins, and a host of other odds and ends to mark the presence of men. The dreams of mineral riches did not die and continued tempting and tantalizing others to come. Even William Byers succumbed.

The Sierra San Juan is the highest, roughest, broadest and most abrupt of all of the ranges. It is from all appearances, and from all the knowledge we are able to obtain, both from our own observations, and the testimony of others, probable that in this range the metaliffrous development of this region, if not of the North American continent, reaches its culminating point.

14

CHAPTER 3
BIRTH OF A MINING TOWN

As the decade of 1860s closed, the lingering aftermath of the 1861 disappointment receded and prospectors reappeared along the Dolores and Mancos rivers. As the summer of 1870 dawned, they returned to Baker's Park. They would only be there seasonally for the moment, coming when weather and snow permitted, prospecting, and getting out before the winter storms closed the passes.

The major problem, besides isolation and lack of development money, persisted—the San Juans remained Ute land. The prospectors and those who followed them trespassed; therefore, they had no legal basis to stake claims or work their mines. The Utes objected. The miners protested. Unenviably trapped between treaty provisions and angry taxpayers, the Federal government looked for a peaceful solution. When mining clashed with native peoples, something had to give way. The pattern remained clear in the first clashes, from California to Alaska—the government sided with taxpayers, even if it involved some effort to protect Indian rights.

Arrastra Gulch where some of the first mines were located.
(Courtesy: U.S. Geological Survey.)

15

Mining pushed the issue to a quick resolution. The Brunot agreement of 1873 ceded the San Juans, giving the prospectors the right to stake and work their claims. That finally opened the San Juans. Gradually during each season in the 1870s, more people arrived and saw mineral potential in these mountains. These pioneer San Juaners were determined to stake the "mother lode," and there seemed to be an abundance of mineralized veins on which to stake one's fortune.

They made some promising discoveries. The Little Giant mine, located at the head of Arrastra Gulch, was the first in 1870. With reported assays running in the $1,000 to $4,000 a ton in gold, that mine aroused great interest. Others followed. Soon silver attracted attention as much as gold, but the San Juaners lacked the finances to develop either. Mountainous isolation and the high elevation troubled them as well. That old mining saying might have encouraged them: the "higher the silver mine, the richer the silver." This seemed true at times elsewhere, particularly at the Potosi mine in Bolivia, but no rich strikes would be made on the tops of local 14,000-foot peaks.

Weather and the short season hindered the seasonal mining efforts; what the miners needed were support bases for year around work. Mining gave birth to an urban west. The frontier of a few people slowly settling a region (agriculture, for example) disappeared before the rush and transitory, fast paced development of mining. Mines and small mining camps could be born and die within a season or two. Yet people came to "mine the miners," because they had, in theory, gold and silver to buy goods and services.

Into the San Juan world of the mid-1870s settlements came. Small mining camps with a few log buildings strung out along an illy-defined dirt main street, a saloon or two, a general store, a blacksmith shop, and perhaps a boarding/rooming house appeared as if by magic. They clung to alpine meadow and river valley, each little hamlet convinced it would grow to become the San Juan metropolis or at the very least, to dominate its own district.

How many might have been stillborn, passing without notice

A prospecting camp in 1875 0n King Solomon Mountain high above Cunningham gulch.
(Courtesy: U.S. Geological Survey)

and mourned only by their promoter-fathers, will never be known. In the peak years of 1874-75, like mountain flowers, a fresh crop blossomed every spring; the less hardy ones faded within a season. It was a dog-eat-dog urban world, as each struggled to promote itself and grow into its dreams. No middle ground sanctuary existed. The losers became ghost sites, and the winners prospered while their mines prospered.

Into this feisty, unforgiving urban world came Silverton in 1874. The origin of that name remains a mystery. Silver coming to the forefront probably accounts for the choice. Apparently, the settlers in the camp voted on their favorite, and Silverton won.

The newborn camp already had a rival, Howardsville, north up the valley a couple of miles. Howardsville, at the mouth of Cunningham Gulch and Stony Pass (a popular, if rugged route into the San Juans), had the early advantage. The 1874 Territorial Legislature designated it as the county seat of newly created San Juan County. At that time, the county was the entire southwestern corner of the territory. In 1876, La Plata County was split from San Juan; eventually Ouray and other counties would be created as mining spread throughout the region.

By that time, the future of Howardsville was sealed. Silverton's movers and shakers had parlayed their own ambitions and vigor into overtaking their neighbor. Aggressively, they enticed, then persuaded, the owners of a smelter and a sawmill to build in young Silverton. Now, nearby San Juaners came to Silverton for lumber and ore processing, both key industries for mining's survival. Silverton's future looked bright, while Howardsville's dimmed. Then Silverton forced an election to decide the county seat designation and, in 1874, won. Silverton received 183 votes of the 341 ballots cast for five different locations in San Juan County.

To overcome their isolation in the heart of the San Juans (one visitor remarked that "one feels as if he is eventually shut out from the rest of the world as there seems no way out"), ambitious Silvertonians launched a road-building program. They quickly finished a trail to the lower Animas Valley, where farmers and ranchers settled to provide foodstuffs and meat for hungry mountain folk. Road building was fine, but only a stopgap measure to await that nineteenth century marvel, the railroad.

Silverton's location also benefited the young community. In a wide valley featuring plenty of expansion room, with natural, though rugged, outlets in several directions, and three potential water sources, it stood ready to take on rivals. The hospitable location was lower and more sheltered than most nearby rivals, although not as near the mines as some of them.

Silverton now had gained the county seat and all the prestige and business that went with that designation. For the future of the community, only a few things proved more important. Almost all of the San Juan mining towns that survived into the 1990s are, or were, county seats. With industry, mines, transportation and the county seat, Silverton was positioned to evolve from mining camp status to a mining town.

The difference was noticeable to visitor and resident alike. Mining towns were larger in population, and had a more specialized business district (clothing and grocery stores, meat markets, doctors, lawyers and so forth). Their architecture ranged from frame to brick

PROSPECTING ON THE UTE RESERVATION—AN OMINOUS MEETING.—Drawn by W. A. Rogers.

To eastern readers (Harpers Weekly) this was a supposed meeting between the Utes and a well dressed prospector.   (Courtesy: Author)

stone/construction.   Nearby mines tended to be richer than those of neighboring camps. Finally, a certain spirit existed, hard to define, but recognizable among the town's populace—a jauntiness, confidence, and optimism that did not fit well around a mining camp.

In the 1870s, Silverton marched steadily ahead. Silverton folks, like those elsewhere throughout the mining west, desired to recreate the life they had left behind. They did not relish the thought that they were living in a frontier epic. They wanted to bring, when possible, the trappings of culture and civilization.

They wished, for example, to have churches and ministers come.   Schools were important too, even if teachers were paid low wages; most of them were women and equal pay for equal work came far in the future.   It was important, also, that frame buildings replaced log structures. A baseball team provided the same ambiance, particularly as a notable addition to help celebrate the Fourth of July.

The year 1876 was the centennial of the United States, and

Colorado would within the twelve months be welcomed as the thirty-eighth state. Silverton celebrated the occasion in fine style. The day opened with anvils pounding, fire crackers poping, and the stars and stripes fluttering on a sixty-foot flagpole. The traditional reading of the Declaration of Independence was followed by a speech, then the residents turned to sports. Horse and foot races took up the early afternoon concluded by a baseball game (alas, they never recorded the outcome). The day concluded with a ball at the building that served as the school-courtroom. Even a band was organized for the occasion. Silverton, in its eyes, had arrived!

Having made strides in the physical appearance of the budding town, Silvertonians turned to organizing the substance, city government. The first five ordinances dealt with the town seal, officers, business licenses, breach of peace, and "an ordinance concerning ordinances." They wanted government, but not expensive, nor too much (only three standing committees) government. They got their wish. Specific civic actions showed the times were changing, however, when the people petitioned "[prayed] the board to restrict dance houses within certain limits," they were horrified that the board defeated it! This was followed by ordinances regarding prohibiting the sale of liquor to minors, dogs (always a problem), and fire prevention. They even got around to purchasing pamphlets to help promote their community. Nothing exceptional in all this, other mining and towns passed similar rules and regulations. The urban mining West did not waste too many minutes!

Despite all these efforts, some visitors failed to see the future shining through the present. Ben Marsh worked in and around the area in 1875. "Rents are high here—$40 for a house with two good rooms. This is a very cold, wet, stormy and disagreeable country to live in. It rains nearly every day in summer and snows nearly all winter." He did praise the "box" buildings under construction as a "pretty good class of that kind." And he told his wife, "The women are all virtuous here so far as I know."

Prominent mining engineer James Hague arrived on a rainy September evening in 1876 and complained that, in this "comfortless

20

Opening transportation routes throughout the San Juans proved a continuing 19th century problem. This one eventually connected Silverton and Ouray. *(Courtesy: Author)*

place," there was "no decent spot to stop in at a hotel." After a day's rest, and finding the Earl House "a very comfortable and good place," Hague's opinion improved. It seemed a "pretty new town" to him, all "frame & log houses." He walked around the camp, not a long hike, and found it had "several stores, taverns, whisky mill, billiards and one considerable smelting works—Green & Co." The camp, Hague noted, "is said to contain 300-400 people in the summer."

By the end of the seventies, Silverton had built a foundation from which to launch its drive to dominate the local urban scene. Howardsville, Eureka, Neigorsville, and other little rivals never recovered, becoming satellite camps to their larger neighbor. Their day had passed, almost before it got started.

Local mining had not kept pace. Of the three factors necessary for a major mining district—high grade ore, best possible transportation, and money for development—Silverton's mines had only the first. Locals had promoted as best they could. The San Juan Mines (1879 pamphlet) boldly claimed a population of "about" 1,000 for Silverton. It listed a very impressive business district for this "supply center," along with the popular newspaper, the La Plata Miner. Offhandedly the publication mentioned that Silverton had "perhaps a half dozen saloons," a fact miners enjoyed, though investors might not think that a positive feature.

Just when it seemed that Silverton might be turning the corner toward success, silver in Leadville exploded on the scene. The San Juans initially could not compete; in the end, though, Leadville brought investors, attention, and promotion to all of Colorado. At the moment, the San Juans languished as a bridesmaid, not a bride.

The arrival of Colorado's silver millionaire, Horace Tabor, with his Leadville-based fortune, cheered San Juaners. Tabor, synonymous with success in Colorado mining, purchased the Alaska mine and others at the head of Poughkeepsie Gulch. In the summer of 1879, he toured the area, being accorded as nearly a triumphal reception as the San Juans could give. Tabor did nothing to dampen the enthusiasm, when he described his property as "worth nearly or about the same now, I suppose, as my interests in Leadville [worth several million]." San Juaners hoped that "where the big fish go, the small fry all follow." That would not come to pass for a while.

The long mountainous, narrow trails, hardly worthy to be called roads, raised the cost of living and the cost of mining, and also handicapped investors to come and see the mines. Limited to seasonal use, and always affected by the volatile mountainous weather, these primitive trails were not the desired answers. As one disgusted San Juaner wrote about the 1876 roads, "After we left Lake City, we traveled over some of the worst road I have ever seen. Only the trees, stumps and rocks which could make the road absolutely impassable had been removed, but no thought had been given to the comfort of the traveler." Improvements helped, as did toll roads, despite grumbling over charges, but the answer remained the railroad.

Patience was required to solve these problems; impatience only made matters worse. By the end of the decade, both the San Juans and Silverton could look back on a successful decade. Maybe not what they envisioned five or seven years before, but worthy of praise. Permanent, year-round settlement had been carved out of the wilderness. An urban support network supported the miners, and a semblance of Victorian respectability had been established. Claims had been staked (far more than would ever be profitable), and mines were opening. Reduction works had been built, although not always answering the needs of the miners. Both the town and its mines could look forward to even a more successful and prosperous decade with the coming of 1880.

CHAPTER 4

MEN TO MATCH THE MOUNTAINS

Miners—they are the ones who opened and developed the San Juans. Who they actually were has been mostly lost to history, but collectively no group proved more significant to Silverton. These men risked their lives daily in the physically taxing, labor intensive profession of mining. Their skills and their labor developed the mines, for which they "received damn little pay" and led a dangerous, shortened life. Look at the cemeteries throughout the San Juans to see how many died in accidents and mining related illnesses, such as miners' consumption that attacked the lungs and left the miner susceptible to a host of more grave illnesses.

Once the poor man's diggings of the gold placer days passed, experienced hard rock miners became essential to Silverton mining. They had to have a "nose" for ore, understand how to drive adits, drifts, and shafts, timber a mine, and handle explosives. In the words of an 1870s San Juan minister, they were "largely young men" and the "majority were intelligent, enterprising and plucky." At this time, many hoped to make enough money to then be able to prospect to stake their own claim to develop a mine. The majority were single because of their occupation, one that insurance companies hesitated to insure. So they joined fraternal organizations that at least provided burial policies.

They arrived from throughout the Rocky Mountains, but the best of them came from Cornwall, England, the Cousin Jacks of mining folklore and legend. The skilled, experienced miner proved essential to opening, developing, and profitably working a mine. He could make or break a mine's success.

In the fast paced, transitory life of mining, miners would work, then tramp off to some more promising district. Others would tramp in to take their place, season after season. Their pay was $3 per day ($3.50 in a wet mine) of which a dollar went back to the company for room and board, unless they lived near the mine. He probably knew

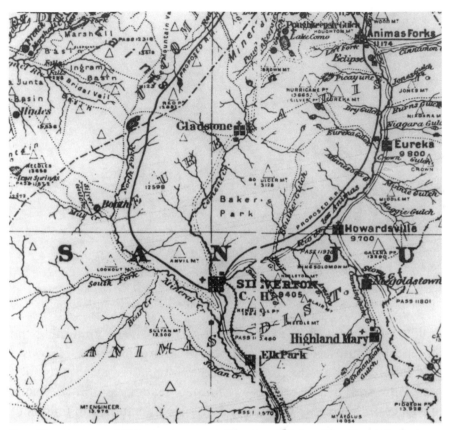

Map Silverton area, 1876 map   (Courtesy: Center of Southwest Studies)

the owner in the early days; perhaps the owner had been a fortunate miner and understood the "in's and out's" of the industry.

For at least the first twenty years of Silverton's mining development, miners had the opportunity to go out on their own or they could "tramp" to another more promising district. This was a safety valve for the miner, who saw the stockholders or owners making a sizeable profit off his dangerous work. That door started to close, however. Soon the miner found machines taking his place and himself little more than a daily worker, whom management often did not value as a skilled professional. Fewer and fewer new districts also opened.

The possibility to become an independent owner decreased

The North Star mine on King Solomon Mountain, high above Silverton, had a checkered career. Elevation was a problem facing all San Juan mines and miners. (Courtesy: Author)

rapidly after the 1880s, as corporations took over mining and the miner found himself only a small part of an organization. He was a paid laborer, not a valued and trusted companion. Also, the most promising sites had already been claimed, leaving him little chance to successfully venture out on his own. He thus turned to unions to represent him in this newly impersonal world. That would lead to trouble after 1900.

The miner's occupation became more specialized as the years went by. For example, there were shift bosses, machine men who operated drills, muckers who loaded the ore cars, trammers who took the cars to the surface, timbermen, station tenders, blasters, mining engineers, and a host of surface workers, including carpenters, hoist operators, blacksmiths, and common laborers. Each was paid a different wage scale, depending on their role, and the workers on the surface usually worked an hour longer each day. The underground workers had to go to work and come out on their own time.

Alva Short worked at several Silverton mines to make the money he needed to start farming. Years later he remembered vividly his mining days, when youth made it seem easy.

Most of my work was tramming. They [Gold King Mine] had a mule there and they had about seven cars that you would take into the mine and load the ore from the chute, and bring them out and dump them at the tipple.

There were all types of nationalities there, most every type you can mention I guess, quite a few Italians. It was a very good place to work, the work wasn't hard and you only worked for eight hours a day.

He also worked as a mucker in the Silver Ledge Mine. "Well you had to shovel. The miners blocked it out pretty well, where you could handle it with a shovel. Be some chunks maybe a foot thick, but lots of it was not too large. You had to shovel it into chutes."

San Juan miners in the 1870s. Isolated, hard working in a dangerous job, and often unwashed, these men opened the region and helped bring about permanent settlement.
(Courtesy: Author)

Other men ran the tramways that spread like spider webs throughout the San Juans or worked in the smelters and mills. In 1896, this amounted to 1,351 men in San Juan County and more than 1,600 five years later. The economic impact of all these miners, plus the supplies, equipment, and so forth needed to operate a mine, provided the foundation for continued settlement and growth for the county and Silverton.

Silverton's business and entertainment sections depended on these men, who came into town on holidays, on days off if they lived close enough, and when they had saved up enough money to have a "fling" in town. They needed relaxation from a job in which they risked their lives every day they went to work.

San Juan miner/poet Alfred Castner King well understood the dangers of mining. Blinded by a premature mining explosion in March 1900, he wrote in his poem "The Miner":

But the arms that deliver the sturdy stroke,
Ere the shift is done, may be crushed or broke,
Or the life may succumb to the gas and smoke,
Which the underground caverns fill.

Clink! Clink! Clink!
The song of the hammer and drill!
As he toils in the shaft, in the stope or raise,
'Mid dangers which lurk, but elude the gaze
His nerves with no terrors thrill.

CHAPTER 5

"QUEEN OF SILVER LAND"

The hope of the 1870s became the reality of the 1880s for the San Juans and Silverton, when the Denver & Rio Grande Railroad arrived and iron rails tied Silverton to the world.. Colorado's "baby railroad" had been planned as a north-south feeder line for the east/west transcontinental railroads. Its president, William Jackson Palmer, hoped to go all the way to Mexico. Then came the Leadville silver boom and conflicts with the Santa Fe Railroad; they managed to turn him, and his narrow gauge three-foot line, into the Colorado Rockies, seeking his own transportation bonanza in the booming mining districts.

For the Silverton and San Juan miners, the 1870s were a decade of waiting for investors to come, for lower mining and living costs, and, most of all, for better transportation to provide desperately needed cheaper, year-round, faster shipping. The railroad offered the potential to solve most of these problems. Silverton folks

Silverton, replete with board sidewalks, children, and frame homes was showing signs of evolving into the "old" home left behind.　　　*(Courtesy: Colorado Historical Society)*

29

had no doubts that their district contained an abundance of minerals that would make it one of the Rocky Mountains' great mining regions, if they could only get a railroad connection.

In late 1879 the world looked brighter than ever before to isolated, mountain-locked Silverton. D&RG surveyors were at work in the Animas Canyon; the wonder of the age was about to challenge the San Juans. The editor of the La Plata Miner (December 29) could not restrain himself: Silverton, "queen of the Silver land," was about to begin a "boom for this country that would not cease growing for a hundred years to come." Three weeks before, the same newspaper had observed, "in fact, it is impossible to estimate the great advantage in every way the completion of this road will be to our camp."

Silverton and its future were about to meet. The nineteenth century town with railroad connections had a bright future with seemingly unlimited potential. The town without a railroad faced considerable obstacles to success, perhaps fatal to the "grow or die" attitude popular with town fathers and boomers.

It would not be an easy courtship. For years, people had envisioned a railroad breaching the mountain barrier, but lack of local mining development, a shortage of railroad finances, and the problems of engineering delayed the arrival. Even surveying crews faced almost insurmountable troubles. They had to be belayed on ropes down canyon walls to complete their work. And the coming of the iron horse would not be an unmixed blessing.

The farming community of Animas City, forty-three miles south of Silverton as the crow flies, (and longer by mountain road), became embroiled in a debate about its future with the D&RG. The little hamlet had been started because of mining. With a longer growing season, plenty of farming land, and abundant water, farmers and ranchers settled to tap the mining market. Now a crisis developed.

The city fathers refused to meet the railroad's terms during the winter and spring of 1879-80 and the D&RG did what it had done before: it threatened to launch a rival community. The La Plata Miner watched with interest. It reported on December 20 that railroad officials were busy buying up townsite and coal lands in anticipation of locating a new community two miles below Animas City. The company town, the editor forecast, would "knock the stuffing out of the present town, yet it will be a good thing for us all, and especially our San Juan neighbors." Envisioning itself a railroad/mining center, Silverton did not want anything to stand in its way. If it cost a neighbor its future, so be it.

That December 20 forecast could not have been more accurate. The two parties never resolved their differences, resulting, on September 13, 1880, in driving the first survey stake for the new town of Durango. Animas City never recovered. Durango, by Christmas 1880, had over 2,000 residents, while Animas City lost its bank, newspaper, and many residents to its upstart rival.

Soon Durango became the regional smelter center, with its San Juan and New York smelter providing the most advanced technology available. Silverton paid a price for this. It lost its Greene Smelter to its downriver rival. Mining and railroad man John Porter and others purchased the mill, dismantled it, and sent it to Durango, where it became the nucleus of the new works. Durango had coal and easier access to the outside world to obtain flux and needed supplies, and hauling ore down hill was easier than anything for a smelter up hill. All this happened before the rails even reached Silverton. The railroad would prove a mixed blessing for the mining town.

Silverton would never free itself from Durango. The two would be locked together at two ends of a railroad, with Silverton at the wrong end for dominance. Durango briefly held title to the largest town on Colorado's Western Slope, only to be passed by Grand Junction at the turn-of-the-century. Few tears were shed, however; Durango emerged as the region's smelting, business, banking, medical, and a tourist center. The railroad's town, named after Durango, Mexico, where it once intended to go, boomed just as the D&RG had forecast.

Silverton watched and waited as the "plucky road" attempted to advance into the San Juans. The D&RG reached Durango in July 1881; officially, the first train, delayed a day by a washout, arrived on August 5. Silverton's baseball team came down to participate in the festivities but lost the game 10-3. Durango had traveled to Silverton for a game on the Fourth, and it won there too, 11-7. Silvertonians "are willing to try another round," boasted the local paper after the Fourth, but the result proved the same. Both teams eagerly awaited the railroad to ease the time and trouble of horse and wagon travel; so did everybody else.

Continuing past Durango, the D&RG built as far as Rockwood, seventeen miles north, before winter closed in and ended construction. For one brief season, that little camp enjoyed a boom as the end-of-the-track supply point. The following spring, the D&RG encountered its most difficult terrain, the "high line," immediately beyond Rockwood. A narrow shelf had to be blasted out of the granite cliffs to hold the rails. Skeptics thought the railroad would never recover its money, because it cost more than a thousand dollars a foot to blast it out. Overcoming that obstacle, the D&RG moved on, and the first train steamed into Silverton in July 1882. As the La Plata Miner (July 15, 1882) observed, "So far, all that can be done by the outside world has been done, for by this medium it has opened to us—what now remains is for us to do—to commence to make ourselves and made good our statements."

The San Juan Herald (July 6, 1882) was even more exhilarated: Silverton, the "Gem City of the Mountains, the most prosperous and promising camp in the entire San Juan," was the "center of the richest mineral area on the face of the earth." The excitement could hardly be contained, but, as the Miner suggested, it was now up to Silverton to prove itself.

Already, Silverton was well on its way to doing that. One thing every mining town had to have was newspapers, and Silverton, during the 1880s, was blessed many times over. In the feverish world of mining, it was essential to have papers to promote, defend, agitate, and motivate. In this personal journalist era an outspoken, colorful editor seemed almost a must. Did the town need both to be defended and have an outspoken editor? Let Ouray's feisty Dave Day prove why on both counts. Silverton, he explained in his Solid Muldoon (April 27, 1883), was having a "boom. We saw it going in

When the Denver & Rio Grande railroad arrived in July 1882, an era closed and another opened. Without a railroad neither the community nor it's mines had much of a future. (Courtesy: Author)

a few days since—three gamblers, two women, and a yeller dog." Silverton papers answered in kind. The streets of Silverton "present a lively appearance now-a-days," proclaimed the San Juan in April 1887, "while poor Ouray still howls for a railroad."

Nor could any one paper expect to have the field all to itself. For example, Silverton during the decade offered readers thirteen dailies and weeklies at one time or another. Some were mergers, a few were daily and weekly editions of the same paper, and others were short-lived, a year or less. No guarantees existed in this hectic newspaper world. The two with the longest existence, the Silverton Miner and the Silverton Standard, eventually merged into the oldest consistently publishing newspaper on Colorado's Western Slope, the Silverton Standard and the Miner.

Silverton got the journalistic jump on all of its neighbors and never relinquished that lead. Never at a loss to promote itself and its mines, the community relished a good newspaper scrape, locally or regionally. Attacks from the outside (Denver, Leadville or beyond), however, would rally all the papers to the common defense. Outside criticism was not welcomed, despite what locals might say about each other.

Silverton's "cup runneth over" in another respect, railroads. Before the 1880s slipped into history, the toll road builder, politician, and mine owner, Russian born Otto Mears, who might have been short in stature but a giant in his Silverton significance, constructed the Silverton Railroad. It went north to tap the prospering silver mines in the Red Mountain district in 1887-88.

The Silverton Railroad returned great profits initially, but too steep grades and the snow slide danger stymied Mears, as he tried to build onto Ouray. Finally, the economic crash of 1893 and the crushing depression ended any dreams of going on northward. Mears, however, had already built the Rio Grande Southern (1890-91) from Durango to Ridgway, tapping Rico's and Telluride's mines and the tourist potential of Mesa Verde along the way. By doing this, he reached Ouray, but it took him over 170 miles to bridge a nine-mile canyon and valley.

Mears was not finished. In 1895 he organized the Silverton Northern Railroad that eventually built north to Howardsville, Eureka, and, by 1904, Animas Forks. He would ultimately gain control of the Silverton, Gladstone and Northerly Railroad (built in 1899). Silverton now had four narrow gauge lines; it was a "narrow gauge capital." Mears operated them, but they all were subservient to the one connecting link, the D&RG. These little railroads reached out to camps and districts within Silverton's economic hinterland. Silverton had achieved the dominance it wanted.

Silverton had become the commercial, social, and transportation hub for a region roughly 108 square miles, rich in gold, silver, lead, copper, and zinc. Included in its little kingdom were the tiny mining camps of Animas Forks, Ironton, Gladstone, Eureka and Chattanooga. Let no rival dare trespass or "war" might break out. This became particularly evident in the Red Mountain district, where Ouray and Silverton hotly competed until Mears' railroad tipped the balance in favor of Silverton. One disgusted San Juaner said a pox on both: "a great deal of unnecessary wrangling is being indulged in by local papers" over the Red Mountain mines. Newspapers blustered, merchants competed, freighters struggled, but Silverton emerged triumphant, thanks to Otto Mears and his Silverton Railroad.

Silverton's mines also prospered. Like the rest of the San Juans, the eighties emerged as the silver decade. Despite a declining price for the metal, San Juan County's silver production jumped over the $100,000 range and twice topped $700,000. Total production that never before had reached $100,000, three times soared above one million dollars with silver leading the way followed by lead, gold, and copper, in that order. San Juan County mining had come of age.

It might have come of age, but the necessary investors still tended to go elsewhere rather than to the San Juans. First Leadville had lured them, then Aspen, in the 1880s, appeared much more accessible and attractive. Silverton was still the bridesmaid, locals could only wait.

Wait, they might, but they would not run out of that faith and optimism as well that fueled the mining west. The Silverton Weekly Miner, January 4, 1890, reviewing the past year, illustrated that fact wonderfully. New strikes were taking place in all parts of the county, the reporter noted. Yet more importantly, San Juaners appeared to have taken a fresh start in prospecting. "Instead of just silver ores," they invariably were finding gold. The result "is many valuable gold discoveries have been made." At least in their eyes, they proved "valuable." San Juaners of this generation never lagged when it came to believing in a better tomorrow.

With railroad connections, improving mineral production, a prospering hinterland, and a vocal cadre of booster/defender newspapers, Silverton matured significantly in the 1880s. A visitor wrote in September 1880 that Silverton "is gradually beginning to enjoy the inevitable results of its advantageous position." Having toured the whole San Juans, he felt that there existed "a greater show of solid wealth and more to be seen on its streets than any other town in the San Juan." Silvertonians loved to read such comments. Their community-image soared over the concluding remark that Silverton "to me at least stands preeminent among the cities of the great San Juan."

Two years later, the Denver Tribune (September 21, 1882) did a feature article on the town. A booster local could not have presented his or her community better. After commenting that the architecture of Silverton "is very creditable indeed," the writer went on to say that there were about 350 buildings, mostly painted, including a good school house and an elegant church. Business houses and dwellings "that would do credit to Denver" have been and "are being erected." The article positively gushed about the business community. "Perhaps no town in Colorado boasts of more reliable and enterprising class of businessmen, merchants, and bankers," who enjoy a "first class reputation at home and abroad." They were "enterprising and public spirited" and fair, honest, and prompt in their business dealings.

The city founders came in for praise, also. They "look carefully after sanitary matters," and it was not "too much to assert that there is not a healthier or better kept town in the state." The reporter also praised the locals. "The class of people composing the permanent residents...are a higher and better class and order than usually found in mining camps."

All these things were what Silverton folks loved to say and write about themselves and their town, now thought of as a "city." An up-to-date, progressive town government and a high class of residents—it could not have been said better. Churches, schools, county court house, substantial architecture, and a prominent business district were all evidence that Silverton had "arrived" and had recreated "Victorian life and society." Potential investors and future residents would love to know what kind of community Silverton had grown into, and this article gave them a very positive image. As the La Plata Miner (September 10, 1881) observed, it was important "to make use of every effort" to make the town a most attractive and desirable place to live.

Burro trains were a familiar sight in Silverton in the nineteenth century. Notice the false fronted buildings so common throughout the West. *(Courtesy: San Juan County Historical Society)*

This "reliable and enterprising" group included, by mid-decade, grocers, bankers, druggists, butchers, assayers, furniture dealers, contractors, newsdealers, clothing merchants, and barbers. There were also hotels, saloons, restaurants, livery stables, a bath house, a transportation company and real estate and insurance agents. Physicians, attorneys, and mining and civil engineers comprised the professional group. They totally represented a very respectable and representative business community, one that would have been quite acceptable for an established midwestern farm town. Nevertheless, when considering Silverton was less than fifteen years old, this signaled to one and all an outstanding achievement. Nothing more clearly showed the attraction and rapid growth of a mining community.

Silverton's population steadily increased, especially with the coming of the D&RG. A state census in 1885 counted 1,195 in the town, a figure that stayed fairly stable until the turn of the century. Another three to four hundred miners worked within easy travel distance of Silverton. These people were mostly Midwestern and northern European stock, with an increasing number of younger Coloradans.

As the 1890s dawned, Silverton had established the foundations for permanency—county seat, transportation hub, mining and business growth, and prospering hinterlands. In doing that, Silverton had surpassed most of its contemporary western mining towns and camps. Even yet, however, no guarantee existed of achieving that elusive goal of permanence. The 1880s had built upon the 1870s and placed the community in a much better situation than it had been a decade before. The future looked promising. Optimism and expectation proved contagious in mining camps and towns.

COLORADO

AREA OF MAP

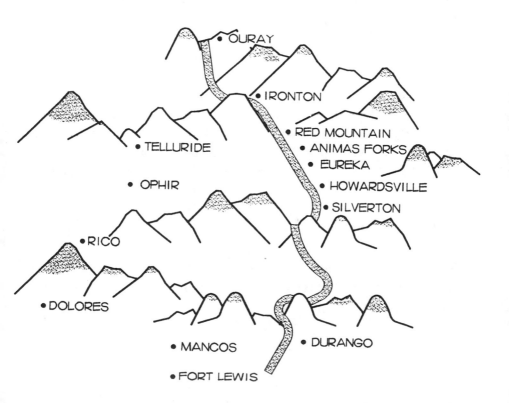

• MONTROSE

• RIDGWAY

• OURAY

• IRONTON

• RED MOUNTAIN
• ANIMAS FORKS
• EUREKA
• HOWARDSVILLE
• SILVERTON

• TELLURIDE

• OPHIR

•RICO

•DOLORES

• MANCOS

•FORT LEWIS

• DURANGO

CHAPTER 6

PARLOR AND CRIB

The parlor and the crib, the home and the children, topped the apex of the Victorian woman's life. Here she entertained and reared her family. The parlor house and the crib symbolized the heart of the Red Light District, the miner's entertainment quarter in a mining town. This Victorian dichotomy of word meanings also yielded the alpha and omega of the woman's role in Silverton and all its urban contemporaries.

The Victorian woman (the era was named after England's long reigning Queen Victoria) found herself a second class citizen. In life and in the home, she was idealized and demeaned. "Every woman should marry," epitomized the woman's place and role. Outside the home, they lived in a man's world; the home belonged to women.

While mining remained almost totally a man's domain, women appeared in the San Juans nearly as soon as the prospectors. They pioneered just as the men did, although they brought the refinement and the culture that made the cabin a home and the town a community. Women were second class citizens in the eyes of the law: they did not have the vote, except in school board elections, and found many professions and jobs closed to them. They wielded an influence far beyond the discrimination they faced, however.

They particularly were active in helping establish the church. In Silverton's first winter, for example, John and Susan Eaton opened their home to regular Sunday religious services. That was fine, but a church building proved even better. Here women found a social outlet for their families, they could hold leadership positions denied them outside, and the church could be a hammer for reform. Particularly in advocating Sunday closing for saloons, prohibition, and the general improvement of the town, women and their churches stood in the forefront.

Sunday closing challenged them, an uphill struggle from the start. Sunday was a wide-open business day, one of the best of the week for local merchants. Not that the movers and shakers did not want a church. They did, if for no other reason than the building displayed a progressive sign of community progress. Still, on a Sunday morning, the minister, a male, looked over his flock, made up predominantly of women and their children.

Those early women deserve a great deal of credit for coming into Baker's Park and making Silverton seem more homelike and much more like the towns left behind. When Sarah Elizabeth Taft gave birth to a daughter on July 29, 1875, it was an event to be remembered. Twenty-five year old Sarah had arrived by mule pack train the year before, after briefly stopping at Lake City. She and her husband, Byron, operated a boarding house for a few years, then moved on, following their dreams.

Nineteen-year-old Zaidee Rockwood's dream ended in 1879, when she died of complications after giving birth; her daughter survived. Pioneering life has often been romanticized, but Zaidee's brief life illustrated more truthfully what faced the pioneer women who journeyed west.

A group of Silvertonians, maybe on a picnic, with their home town behind them.
(Courtesy: San Juan County Historical Society)

One thing a mining community provided for Sarah, Zaidee, and their pioneering sisters was more feminine companionship than would have been available for years on the farming frontier. Another thing the masculine-dominated world of mining supplied was fewer social restraints. A bad marriage might have to be endured back east, but not as often in Silverton, where there were many available men and little social stigma for a "grass widow." More jobs also opened, as women could move more easily into male-dominated businesses. Still, though, women's main role remained in the home as wife and mother.

Typical of the women who came and made Silverton their home was Una McCoin Hinkley. She arrived in 1881 as a ten-year-old, attended school, and grew up in Baker's Park. Her first marriage ended in divorce, and in 1908 she married Frank Hinkley, a prominent mining man, who owned one of the first cars in San Juan County. This homemaker and mother saw her only child die in the 1918 flu epidemic. She also saw many changes, from great hopes to boom to decline, in the fifty-three years she lived in Silverton.

Letizia Maffet and her young daughter came to Silverton in 1908 from their native Italy to join her husband, who had immigrated four years before. This was a typical pattern for so many immigrants. Unfortunately, some families never made it to the new world before the husband and father was killed or disappeared.

Like so many women Letizia suffered the loss of a baby six days after his birth. An old Victorian saying existed that the family had to have four children, one for mother, one for father, one for natural increase, and one who would die. Women knew death very intimately during these generations. Active in the community and church, businesswoman Letizia and her husband and daughter operated what became known as the French Bakery for over half a century. She left no particular monument to mark her Silverton years, except that of being a good wife, mother, and resident.

Laura Stoiber and her sister-in-law Helen (she used the name Lena) were much better known in their day. Their husbands became two of Silverton's best known mining men. Originally partners in a

The home of the <u>San Juan Herald</u> in the early 1880s, this building, modified, still stands on Reese St. *(Courtesy : Center of Southwest Studies)*

sampling mill, they owned two famous mines, Silver Lake and the Iowa Tiger. The brothers had been prominent in the town and county since the early 1880s. The two dissolved their association after Lena arrived, she may have caused the dissolution, and, according to Silverton social custom, both families were seldom invited to the same event. The two women did not enjoy each other's company, to say the least, calling each other "that boarding-housekeeper" and "that painted thing."

Laura was much beloved in Silverton; Lena, or Captain Jack, was not. Their personalities contrasted—Laura friendly, popular, and active in the community, Lena, strong willed, with a fiery temper, capable of both kindness and fury. The latter got along with only a few people and was "not on speaking terms" with many more. The two couples lived across Reese Street from each other, until Lena built her famous mansion, Waldeim, north of town in 1895. Laura represented Silverton's social "upper crust." Lena was a hard driving businesswoman, who worked with her husband, Ed. She fought

They called it snowshoeing in the 19th century, we call it skiing.
(Courtesy: Silverton Standard and the Miner)

arduously to save Mesa Verde, however, and make it a national park. Both became Silverton legends in their day.

English born Jane Bowen, locally known as "Sage Hen," lived in a different part of Silverton than the Stoibers. She, too, was a legend and a "painted thing" without question, the owner of a popular dance hall on Blair Street in Silverton's Red Light District. She and her husband together operated a saloon and dance hall.

Legendary in its day, and today as well, Silverton's Red Light District contributed an important element of the town's business district. The saloons, parlor houses, cribs, dance halls, and "low class"

44

variety theaters that went up to make this mining community institution beckoned miners to come and provided many stories for the local press.

Silverton, like other towns including Durango, passed ordinances against gambling and prostitution, then allowed them to flourish and collected monthly fines. Both Rose Atwood and Mildred Mason, for instance, were fined $19.75 and costs in early January 1902 "for being an inmate in a bawdy house." Phillie Edwards got off easier, $14.75 for "breach of the peace and fighting." That way the city fathers kept taxes lower and proved that "you could have your cake and eat it too!"

There was nothing romantic about the Red Light District. It was all business. It also was the source of much of the town's lawlessness and drunkenness, drugs, "social diseases," and abortions. As early as 1877, citizens petitioned the Council about such nuisances as dance halls, "praying the board to restrict dance houses within certain limits." They eventually accomplished that, but a mining community had to allow the Red Light District to operate, because it was good for business generally. Recreation-seeking miners would go somewhere else nearby if no brothel was open locally, and it hurt all of Silverton. Interesting, too, was the image that this district remained part of a "real" mining town. Visitors then, like tourists today, enjoyed seeing or reading about the "sin" that normally did not appear in their life back home.

It took an astute business woman to survive in this atmosphere, and Jane Bowen matched the challenge. Popular with the denizens of her district, she and her contemporaries were not welcome to associate with the "good ladies." She worked off and on in Silverton until past the turn of the century.

Women from all walks of life contributed in various ways to Silverton's history. Individually, their contributions may have been forgotten. Totally, they represent Silverton at its best and sometimes at its worst. Perhaps author George Eliot (pen name for Marian Evans Cross) was right, "The happiest women, like the happiest nations, have no history."

CHAPTER 7

GOLDEN BACKBONE

The 1890s have been often looked upon as "the good old days." If so, the good old days were not that good. Silverton, Colorado, and the nation suffered through a severe economic crash and the worst depression the state and community had suffered. From 1893 until after mid-decade, it hung on and changed Silverton. Some parts of the San Juans never recovered. Along with it came the collapse in the price of silver and the bitter political fight between the gold bugs and the silverites, culminating in the emotional 1896 presidential election. Increasingly, labor unrest pitted the miners against management, and they marched relentlessly toward violence. It was a decade to remember, though, perhaps through rose-tinted glasses.

The silver San Juans, along with all Colorado silver producing districts, had watched since the early 1870s as the price of silver collapsed from a $1.30 per ounce to the 90 cents range by 1890. Buyers paid that amount for the refined product, not for the raw ore that came out of the mine portal.

Predictably, silver miners protested and the "silver issue" was born. They wanted the government to purchase their silver at a guaranteed price of $1.25. Twice, Uncle Sam agreed to purchase silver at the market price and coin it. The second time (1890 Sherman Silver Purchase Act) fifty-four million ounces per year, the assumed total production of the United States, was bought by the Federal government. Nothing seemed to help the price, however, and that remained the vital question.

By the late 1880s, the silver question had swept over Colorado politics. It pitted "honest, hardworking Coloradans" vs. eastern bankers and creditors, silverites vs. gold bugs, rich vs. poor, and East vs. West. Emotions ran high. Logic took a back seat.

"Free Silver" carried the day, and Silverton stood in the front ranks of the fight. The Silverton Standard (July 15, 1893) spoke out—silver was the money of the common people and would win this fight against "usurers and bankers." The gold standard (gold as the base for currency) would aid the "moneyed aristocracy" and "increase pauperism and poverty of the masses." We will have silver coinage because silver money is 'honest money' and for the reason that the surreptitious demonetization of silver twenty years ago [1873] was a crime."

"Let silver drop to 75 cents per ounce and there would not be a silver mine worked in America, and all our western cities would be paralyzed; our rails would cease to pay," warned Horace Tabor. Otto Mears concurred. If Congress did not "do something for silver this year [1893] property will decrease in this state so enormously that it will absolutely ruin every one in it." The men on the street and in the mines of Silverton agreed.

When easterners and others blamed the Sherman Silver Purchase Act for the crash, their Congressmen united to repeal it in the fall of 1893. The silver price collapsed to the fifty cents per ounce range. Silverton wept, and mining in the San Juans collapsed.

In the dark clouds boiling over the mountains, however, there

One of Silverton's three little narrow gauge lines, the Silverton, Gladstone and Northerly. (Courtesy: San Juan County Historical Society)

appeared a golden lining. Reaching into the mountains' mineral treasure box, San Juaners found gold. Gold had brought them into the San Juans before silver seized their attention, now it would rescue them. San Juan County silver production remained high through 1899, in fact, setting a record of more than two million ounces in 1896. Gold mining, meanwhile, steadily increased, topping $1,000,000 in value for the first time in the county in 1898. In the mines, they now mined silver as a by-product, gold as the primary metal. Gold became the backbone, the savior of San Juan County mining.

At last, with adequate transportation and renewed vigor, the San Juans finally came into their own. Only exciting, golden Cripple Creek over by Pike's Peak claimed more interest and headlines.

Gold bailed them out of the depression depths by the end of 1895. A visitor noted in December that "work on gold and silver" mines was "being pushed forward on all sides." New York's respected Engineer & Mining Journal featured several articles on San Juan county mines in 1897. What the Silvertonians loved to read was when authors used such terms as "good grade gold, copper, and silver," high grade gold, employing 115 miners, building a tramway, property in "splendid shape," and shipped ten cars of concentrates.

It was like the "old" days. Prospectors scurried about the mountains and about twelve miles east of Silverton, in the dark days of 1893, struck gold at Bear Creek. "Strikes were reported at all points of the compass." The Gold Run, or Bear Creek, excitement lasted for a season with the usual "big strikes," excitement, and a nascent mining camp at the "great Eldorado of the southwest." Within a year, it had receded from the front page.

The Gold Run excitement offered the ordinary San Juaner another chance to strike it rich. For most people, however, this opportunity had become part of the legend, not the reality of mining. In and around Silverton, and in the entire San Juans, the profitable mines had fallen into the hands of corporations or well-to-do owners. This trend had a variety of implications for both the owners and miners, not the least of which heightened labor tensions. It also marked the coming of the end of an era dominated by graduates of the school of hard knocks. College-trained mining men moved to the forefront, to the dismay of many old-timers. They knew geology, mining engineering, and smeltering, but old-timers were not convinced that this was a step in the right direction.

Individual mines and mining men now came to dominate San Juan County. Edward Stoiber, graduate of the Freiberg School of Mines, was one of the new breed. He, and his brother Gus, had come to Silverton to start a sampling works and operate mines, the best of which was Silver Lake. One of Colorado's leading mining men and metallurgists, Stoiber turned Silver Lake into one of the most modern and economical mining plants in the West.

High above Silverton in Arrastra Basin, the Silver Lake Mine, by 1899, was producing over 6,000 tons of ore each month. That was taken by tram (14,700 feet, one of the longest in the United States) to Stoiber's mill along side the Animas River and the Silverton Northern Railroad. Electricity, telephones with a private line, drilling ma-

Silver Lake crew and cooks. *(Courtesy: Western History Department Denver Public Library)*

chines, and a steam heating plant also showed that mining had changed in the past twenty-five years.

His employees "highly esteemed Stoiber" because, as one article said, "he was always kind and considerate" to them. That was more accurate than the "puff" that was often written about prominent mining men. The four story Silver Lake boarding and bunk house was steam heated, with a reputation for serving excellent food in the dining room. Water was piped in from the upper part of the basin to furnish "healthy water for domestic purposes." "With such accommodations," a "superior class of miners and mill men can be secured," despite a "disagreeable winter climate and high altitude [12,186 feet]."

Mining people came to see the Stoiber operation. Nothing better displayed the fact that San Juan County had finally come of mining age. Nearly as successful and equally esteemed locally was John Terry, who came to the region in the mid-1880s. Fifty-niner Terry had a much harder time getting his Sunnyside mine in operation because of a lack of capital. Involved was one of the oldest claims in the district, and Terry had gained control of the property after a disagreement with the other owners. He eventually built a concentrating plant and a mill at Eureka, as well as a tram from there to his mine 2,500 feet above the little camp. Eureka, a little over four miles north of Silverton, in time, would come to look upon itself as Silverton's rival and, by the era of World War I, would be a prospering camp.

Terry and his sons worked the property and by 1899 had their gold and lead mine producing regularly. These were the types of mines that everyone hoped to find and develop. They proved the exception. Many "mines" never went beyond their owner's dreams; others lasted only a year or two, and most that eventually produced ore only returned small profits. The rich and famous grabbed the headlines. The majority of owners and miners only made a living.

Despite praise for both Terry's and Stoiber's milling operations, local miners were never able to break free from under the Durango smelter. It was the region's best and could handle all types of ore. Locals lamented this development, but it was not all bad.

50

Churches have always played an important role in Silverton. The corner stone for the now United Church was laid in 1880; the church stands on Reese St. (Courtesy: Glen Crandall)

Stoiber, along with other mining men, had bemoaned the loss of money wasted on mills. He had "no patience" with an irrational system that filled "so many gulches with useless milling plants." Optimism outran reality too often, to the dismay of investors and the ruination of mines.

San Juaners could be pleased in two other areas, however—they pioneered in the use of electricity and tramways. Both proved very successful in cutting mining costs. The trams helped overcome elevation and narrow mountain trails. The buckets, strung on cables between towers, made it easier and cheaper to transport ore to the mills, or the railroad, and supplies to the mines. Even miners rode the buckets back and forth on occasion, and injured men could be taken down on special stretchers. Electricity, while expensive, eliminated freighting costs for fuel and provided light for mine, and mill.

Investors arrived, too, now that the train made it so easy. They came from England, the continent, and throughout the United States. Beckoned by the renewed vigor of local mining, they hoped that the property they purchased, or invested in, would reflect the following comment about the industry.

In modern mining the chances are reduced to a minimum. It is conducted by men who know what they are about .... Mining products have a permanent value. This is no waste, nothing to perish. The product of the mines is the basis of all wealth. It is always in demand.

Unfortunately, most found that "wonderful" profits did not follow their investment; they had not found the royal road to wealth. Many of their investments, as one mining reporter noted, "serve only to build monuments of failure, folly, and dishonesty."

Harsh weather, low-grade ore, high elevation, isolation from mill and railroads, mismanagement, over expectations, collapse of the price of silver, mining disputes that ended in the courts, and rising costs of mining—individually or in combination—dashed dreams. Mining did cost more now, as the miners burrowed deeper into the mountains. Ore grades generally declined with depth, thereby compounding the problem.

The changes in mining were reflected down in the valley at Silverton. The townspeople never wavered in their support of the industry nor free silver. If the mines slumped, so did Silverton; if they prospered good times returned. The 1890s were neither the best nor the worst of times.

Unlike newcomer Creede, and a few smaller camps that had a 1890s moment in the sun, Silverton no longer rated as newsworthy as it had been. Twenty years old now, the community had matured. The excitement, the boom, lingered in yesteryear; Silverton had come of age as an established mining town. Foremost, it had survived and grown and already lived longer than many of its contemporaries. It had matched the era's "grow or die" philosophy. The town in Baker's Park had proven the wisdom of its founders and the future still seemed promising despite the hard times of the 1890s.

This maturity was noticeable in many ways. The business district stabilized, and fewer new firms opened. Less journalistic squabbling occurred with neighbors; almost all had reached their business and mining angle of repose. Towns now dominated, as camps declined or became less rambunctious in their pretensions.

Walking down Greene and Blair Streets in 1899, the visitor might have been shocked by number of saloons (nineteen). Not to mention what the reaction may have been to the activities of the rest of the red light district. Otherwise, Silverton looked like many towns of its size with the typical grocery, dry goods, hardware and drug stores, along with bankers, lawyers, physicians, and insurance agents. Merchants were more worried about people buying goods from Sears and Wards catalogues than they were about neighboring towns. They complained that they offered credit to customers who sometimes had not paid for "six months and a year." Customers rebutted that they wanted lower prices and more selection.

While Sunday remained a wide-open business day not turned over to the Sabbath, it was calming down. Church news, good for potential investors and residents to read, was a regular newspaper feature. Rowdiness and the coming and going of the Red Light district's drifting crowd appeared less frequently. When Sunday school outings and activities of the Ladies Aid Society came to be reported regularly, the image of the mining West had changed.

Silvertonians even kept up with the latest fads. Nothing emerged more popular than bicycling in the nineties. The arrival of the bicycle "drummer" in the spring, with new models and gadgets, heralded the season and excited local riders. Salesmen with news, jokes, and wares were always welcome in isolated mining communities. When somebody did something unusual on a bike, like riding over the mountains from Rico in eight hours, it rated comment. So did the fact that some bicyclers were riding on city sidewalks. The city council took notice of this and instructed the marshal to notify riders "to keep off the sidewalks."

Recreation and celebrations took on a more organized form and appearance. Although power drills were replacing hand drillers in the miners, single- and double-jack drilling contests were extremely popular. Drilling against time and competitors, a local champion or team upheld Silverton's honor just as the baseball team did. Betting on the side also enhanced the interest.

Few holidays equaled July 4 in Silverton for community involvement. For example, in 1893, despite economic woes, the town heartily celebrated. A parade, baseball game (Silverton 13, Ouray 3), drilling contests, tug-of-war, burro, horse, and boys' and girls' races were all "witnessed by a large crowd." A fireman's dance, with dancing "kept up until 3 a.m.," crowned the day. "All enjoyed themselves" in a day marred by only one accident, "one little boy lost an eye" in a firecracker accident.

Union veterans, and their Grand Army of the Republic organization, always commemorated fallen comrades on Memorial Day. And because Silvertonians, like Americans overall, were joiners, the town supported a variety of fraternal lodges and societies. It also had a miner's union that sponsored social events and worked to improve health and safety conditions in the mines, better pay, and shorter hours. Not everyone agreed with unions—some thought they were too un-American, radical and violent. Time would tell what would happen.

Two "hot" political issues confronted Silverton voters in the 1890s—woman's suffrage and free silver. When the reform Populist party seized the minds of Coloradans in the 1890s, women had a rare opportunity. The Populists supported giving women the right to vote. Back in 1877, men had defeated a suffrage vote, but now times were different. When the legislature approved a referendum election, hope soared. The women organized, discussed, and worked in 1893 to get the vote out. The liquor interests, fearing prohibition, organized too slowly to stem the "dry" tide, and other opponents remained disorganized. The result, San Juan County joined most of its neighbors and the rest of the state to vote yes. Men in La Plata and San Miguel counties stubbornly voted against the tide. They probably had some explaining to do to their wives and female friends in the days that followed the election!

In the heated, emotional 1896 campaign the local press made its feelings well known. On October 10, the Standard told how it felt about Democratic candidate, Silverite William Jennings Bryan. "As

A parade coming down Greene Street included a multitude of bicycles.
(Courtesy: San Jaun County Historical Society)

he was as he is, as he will be on election day, Bryan is our man, first, last and always." Nor did the Miner lag, "In our next issue we expect to congratulate President Bryan." Back in Colorado, again working over at Telluride, mining engineer James Hague caught the fever of the day. "In Colorado Bryan is regarded as a Moses, a divinely appointed leader of the people, or, at least, a Lincoln, raised up to save and redeem his people."

Alas, the tale would be told, but not like San Juaners expected. Silverton overwhelmingly voted for Bryan over gold Republican William McKinley, 850 to 9, mirroring the pattern of the entire San Juans. Nationally, he lost, free silver had failed. The Standard (November 7) could only console its readers: "Through coercion and the great money powers, Bryan is defeated. The battle was a hard one and was bitterly contested. Time was when principle could hold its own against capital. Will this ever occur again?" That question would occupy the minds of reformers for the next twenty years.

As the decade neared its end, Silvertonians patriotically supported the war against Spain. It lasted such a short time, three months, that they and most other Americans hardly appreciated its signifi-

cance. The "little coming out party" made America a world power.
Some diehards thought the "war may result in the free coinage of
silver"; they did not elaborate just how that might happen.

Already, however, there appeared a yearning for the "old
days." Stories about old-timers, and even ten and twenty years ago
columns, appeared in San Juan papers. The same yearnings were
being expressed when comments like this event or that development
were "not like the old days." The old-timers even took upon themselves an air of distinction and exclusiveness. They organized the
San Juan Pioneers Association, holding annual meetings, for those
pioneers who had arrived "before July 4, 1880." The San Juans and
Silverton were already marching into legend.

CHAPTER 8

SILVERTON'S FIELD OF DREAMS

"Whoever wants to know the heart and mind of America had better learn baseball, the rules and realities of the game," observed philosopher Jacques Barzun. That is true for Silverton and also the rest of the mining west, as well. Baseball arrived in the dust of the pioneers and became Silverton's ultra-ego on the baseball diamond.

The town nine's successes gladdened local folks and probably enriched Blair Street bettors. Not to mention that a victory on the field obviously improved Silverton's self-image. Everybody loved a winner! Defeat, especially to a San Juan rival, brought gloom and despair until a new day dawned.

As mentioned earlier, the first recorded (but no final score reported) baseball game was played on the centennial Fourth of July

A group of visitors to Molas Lake; mountain trips for tourists and locals alike were always popular.   (Courtesy: Author)

in 1876. Without gloves and probably playing on a barely cleared field, it probably ended in a high scoring affair. For instance, a game between two Silverton teams, three years later, ended 36-24 and was followed by a "most amusing race between burros." These early affairs between "picked nines" were hotly contested, but in the 1880s, baseball rivalries with neighboring towns' teams were all the rage. Silverton would take on Telluride, Ouray, Rico, Durango, Lake City, or any of its other neighbors.

In 1881, Silverton suffered those twin defeats at the hands of its newest rival, Durango. On the Fourth of July, they lost at home when the left fielder "muffed" a fly. Durango went on to tie the score and won the contest in six innings, 11-7. At the end of the game "customary cheers were given both clubs and the umpire." The nine went to Durango as part of the train arrival celebration and lost again 10-3.

When the tracks reached Silverton in July 1882, at least travel became easier to away games, with their heated rival at the other end of the line. Ease of travel did not guarantee a better outcome, however. In 1886, Silverton lost to Durango 25-20 for a $75 purse. They redeemed their honor by defeating Fort Lewis 31-17. Some questions about that first game's umpiring emerged. According to the locals, "outside of the base ball game the Durango gentleman who umpired Monday's game appeared to be a very nice fellow but some of his decisions certainly were very rank. He always favored the visiting club."

Silverton and Durango continued their rivalry throughout the years. Over the two-day July fourth holiday in 1903 Silverton defeated Durango's teams three times. Twice the men's team won. "Both teams were in high spirits and came into the field with determination of winning out." Silverton prevailed 13-12 and 12-3. The "juvenile" ball teams played the other game. "But the high altitude played the deuce with the young Durangoites and the score stood 4 to 15."

Not finished, Silverton journeyed to Durango before the month was out. "The crowd that went to Durango Sunday enjoyed the ball

A formidable Silverton nine, plus perhaps the manager and sponsor.
(Courtesy: San Juan Historical Society)

game. Silverton was beaten by a score of 9 to 6 yet it was a good game and was fairly umpired." Then, in mid-August, the team and "nearly seventy" fans returned and beat Durango eight to five, "by far the best game so far this year. There was good playing on both sides, fair umpiring, plenty of rooters and a good natured and happy crowd."

"Fair umpiring" received attention in accounts of these games. Umpiring usually created strong feelings, one way or the other. So did bringing in "ringers" to help the opposition nine. The <u>Silverton Standard</u> (July 19, 1902) took a slap at Ouray after losing to them.

The game at the last half of Silverton's inning stood 12 to 4 in favor of Ouray, or rather in favor of those who played with Ouray's team. It is no further a question of one San Juan town vieing with another in the game of baseball, but a question of what town is capable of securing the best talent from the outside.

The paper strongly championed "that members of nines must be bona fide residents of the respective San Juan towns."

Silverton, however, should not have thrown rocks. When the situation demanded, it could be guilty of the same offense. When Silverton imported a "professional battery" and thumped Durango 25-6, the Herald took the morally high road. "Durango can afford to lose a game of baseball, but Durango cannot afford to win by questionable methods."

Generally, both sides and fans enjoyed themselves, quite often with a picnic, dinner, or some other celebration to top off the day. It helped, of course, to come out a winner. When Silverton defeated Ouray twice, in a Labor Day morning and an afternoon game, "large crowds watched and enjoyed same."

Silverton could crow with the best of them when the nine won. This headline appeared in the Standard, June 28, 1902: "Silverton 16 Ouray 7"

> The above headline conveys the story of Ouray's Waterloo Sunday last when Barnett's 'Braves' went against the real thing in the several and aggregate persons of Slattery's 'Slashers.' Ouray has been going against [the] easy thing in the Ridgway, Telluride and other clubs so long that it was very naturally and pardonably swelled up, but the boys and the other visitors took their defeat in good part and promise at the first opportunity to retrieve the standing of their clubs.

Politician and saloon keeper John "Jack" Slattery was a long time sponsor and supporter of Silverton baseball. A locally famous bon vivant, entrepreneur, and mining investor, he forged some excellent teams.

Ouray, Telluride, and Silverton had a hot rivalry in the 1890s and early 1900s. They were all thriving mining communities, and each wished to be the "queen of the San Juans." The year 1906 saw them about evenly matched. The games reflected better playing surfaces, equipment and, no doubt, more skilled players. Visiting Silverton defeated Telluride 2-1, then won 6-5, for example. At home

With the school in the backround, a group of young women play baseball even if they are using rocks for bases.   (Courtesy: Colorado Historical Society)

and away, Silverton defeated Ouray within one week. Ouray blamed its home loss on poor umpiring!

Not always did a team come forth to champion Silverton. In 1888, however, the <u>San Juan Democrat</u> became concerned, as May neared its end. No team had been formed. There resided, the editor lamented on May 31, "plenty of good baseball players in Silverton. If citizens would only give them proper encouragement a club would be formed." The admonition worked and within two weeks, a "ball club is out practicing" and doing "very well for the short time they have been organized."

Sometimes the town team was supplemented by other local nines. In 1902, the "Rooters and Neversweats" joined the fray. For those who enjoyed playing but were not good enough to make the Silverton team, this offered the perfect answer. In all cases, baseball served as a doorway for the new immigrants to enter, at least partly, the American main stream. Eastern European names, for instance, appeared on teams almost as soon as they arrived in the San Juans. A man's ethnic background or religion did not seem that important;

what mattered was whether he could hit with power, field, or pitch.

Baseball reporting at the time had its own particular flair, little known to modern fans. The Silverton Weekly Miner's game coverage of July 14, 1905 caught the flavor of the game and its meaning to the town. As the reporter noted, "a peculiar feature" occurred in this game. The Glaze boys, "Ralph and Johnny, pitched on opposing sides."

> The much-talked of game between Silverton and Ouray, which took place on the Ouray diamond last Sunday, was a peach. Taking the score, the number of errors and the playing throughout, there are few games in the great leagues which show better playing. The score stood 2 to 0 in favor of Silverton, and both runs were honestly earned. Errors were few. Betting was not as heavy nor as brisk as was expected, although several dollars came over the hill to Silverton as a result of the game.

When America entered World War I, baseball took a back seat to patriotism. Many of the boys were drafted or volunteered, and war news replaced baseball news and many other topics as well. An era ended for the town and its baseball fraternity.

Baseball had said much about Silverton and Silvertonians— the optimism, confidence, and a new season's fresh start reflected mining at its best. Perhaps even the gambling did as well! The enthusiasm of players and fans, the equalitarism of the ball field, and the eternal hope were part of the community's best nature. The game served as an outlet for town pride and a recreational outlet second to none.

Perhaps a fitting epitaph for baseball and Silverton was the obituary of Earl Babcock and his tombstone at Hillside Cemetery. He was remembered as a baseball man, one of Silverton's most popular players in the early part of the twentieth century. There are far worse ways to be remembered. As Mark Twain wrote "to arrive at a just estimate of a renowned man's character one must judge it by the standards of his time, not ours."

Baseball had truly been a "field of dreams" for many Silverton folk. They would not forget the years when they and their community were "marvelously young then wonderfully young."

CHAPTER 9
"A WIDE-OPEN TOWN"

Guy Emerson arrived in Silverton in 1905 looking for a location to start a bank. Even years later, he remembered the times vividly.

So then Silverton was booming, the mills were being built, mines were in operation, they were developing mines I should say, rather than operating. There were two mines, big mines that were operating. The Gold King, the Sunnyside, and I think the One Hundred. I was just carried off my feet with the activity in Silverton. I think they had about 3,000 people there at that time. At night the streets were crowded with people. Mining was the primary industry, but it took a lot of these things [businesses] to run a mining industry.

He became "thoroughly sold on Silverton for another bank." On July 5, 1905, he opened the Silverton National Bank.

After the turn-of-the-century, Silverton boomed. New mining methods and reduction processes, especially the separating and

Sunnyside mine, no. 1 leval, 1902. Underground photographs of early mines are rare because of the use of flash powder to take the picture. *(Courtesy: Allen Bird)*

refining of zinc, gave local mines new life. Emerson had chosen well.

His new home was different from any place he had previously lived, and so were his potential customers. "Unfortunately, the merchants in town were pretty well off. They had money enough to run their own business. Our difficulty, and it was difficult, was to loan money in safe places." The single miners "would stay up at the mine for a month or two or three and then they would come down and have a big time. Spend their money. There wasn't much saving on account of single men there but men with families, of course, they saved their money."

Guy went on to describe his new home. "Silverton was a wide-open town and they had many saloons and a lot of gambling. "I didn't frequent the gambling houses because in the bank, I thought that I ought to stay out of them, but I did know what was going on there." Raised a Southern Methodist, Emerson said, "of course they didn't like drinking and gambling," so young and inexperienced Guy signed a petition to close down gambling. He found out about mining towns. "That was like signing a death warrant with all the people that were depositors in my bank who believed in gambling. I lost a lot of accounts."

Guy Emerson learned that it might be a new century, but tradition and old habits lingered. The new and the old combined, and Silverton prospered as never before. In the years before American entry into World War I, in 1917, Silverton enjoyed its greatest mining boom.

Throughout the entire period, production topped one million dollars per year and, eleven times, it surpassed more than two million. Emerson was right, the Gold King and Sunnyside were two major producers, joined by Silver Lake, which the smelting and mining millionaire Guggenheims had purchased. Each had its own mill or concentrating plant of the most modern type. Only neighboring Telluride and booming Cripple Creek could rival Silverton as major Colorado mining communities and districts. Problems still existed, as they always do in mining. A mining engineer's report on the

Freighting in the mountains in the winter could be a dangerous adventure. It was always costly.   (Courtesy: Author)

Sunnyside Mine in 1906 outlined several troubles hindering Silverton mining. Freight rates were high, "as everything must be brought around a long way on narrow gauge lines." "Not the best" local timber for the variety of mine needs had to be augmented by lumber from "below Durango," which raised the cost to eight to ten cents per foot at the mine. Finally, while the labor scale "is 10-15% lower all around than in Butte," and very much "improved over what it was a year or more ago," the labor force "is mostly foreigners," and "it is by no means safe or trust worthy." To make matters worse, "the Unions are strong."

Indeed, it was "improved." Back in 1903-04, the San Juans— and all of Colorado— had gone through a labor "war." On one side stood the Western Federation of Miners, a hard rock union organized back in 1893. The miners had reacted to the increased corporation dominance of their industry and the corresponding decline in importance of the individual miner. The Western Federation of Miners took root throughout Colorado and won a major strike in Cripple Creek in 1894. It pushed for, among other things, higher wages, the eight-hour day, safety and health laws, and union recognition. There had been weaker local unions in the San Juans before the coming of the WFM, but by the turn of the century, it dominated the labor scene.

On the other side stood management. Owners looked upon unions as a threat to private ownership, violent, anti-American, and denying both the owner and the worker the right to negotiate in the traditional "free market" manner. The Cripple Creek owners had lost, but they and their colleagues throughout the state looked upon the struggle as far from over. On their side, they could count many of Colorado's newspapers, the conservative state courts, the governor, and the national guard. What unfolded was a struggle, a struggle to see who would dominate the San Juans and Colorado mining.

The two major districts, Silverton and Telluride, both contained strong union locals. In Silverton, a local resident remembered union membership as being a prerequisite to working in the mines, and most of the townspeople also joined one or another. Silverton had a miner's union hospital, as did Telluride. From the miners' view, these seemed positive developments. The owners bided their time.

Trouble, when it came, again started in Cripple Creek in 1903 and spread throughout the state. Telluride exploded as it became the San Juan center of the union/management fight. From early fall through the winter of 1904, the two sides squared off. The brutal struggle featured violence, hired gun fighters, deportations, denial of civil liberties, martial law, national guard troops, and curfews. Before it was over, Colorado spent over three-quarters of a million dollars and gained reputation for violence and labor/management hatred.

No question about who won—the well organized and financed

Power drills were introduced in the mines in the 19th century easing work but causing health-undermining dust. Hard hats and other safety equipment came in future years. (Courtesy: Author)

owners carried the day. Silverton had not been in the center of the storm but, financially and physically had loyally supported their union brothers in Telluride. A brief strike at the Gold King mine a year later was a quickly settled aftermath. The Telluride defeat proved a blow to all the San Juan locals, however, and the Silverton local closed its doors in 1910. The goals and ideals of the union did not die, however, they lived on.

Those who lived through those days never forgot. The strike generated hostility that ended an era. The friendship, the freewheeling spirit of an earlier time disappeared in a twinkling.

On a more positive note, the development of electrical power benefited both mines and town. Electricity saved the day for some mines, in fact. The mining engineer, in his 1906 report, noted that the Animas Power & Water Company had just completed a plant below Silverton, and transmission lines were already built up the Animas River to supply the mines. "A very favorable factor into the mining situation about Silverton," he concluded. The San Juans had pioneered in the use of electricity. It lowered fuel and transportation costs and provided a safe, dependable light and power source.

The original, privately owned electric light system broke down during Christmas week demands in both 1902 and 1903. Those annoyances so aroused Silvertonians that they voted bonds for a municipal owned utility and built their own (reportedly, the second AC plant in the country). City Council responded by establishing an electric light department in 1905, with an appropriate ordinance detailing rules, regulations, and costs. The ordinance included a carrot and stick. If bills were not paid "within 10 days, the city would cut off services." Those who promptly paid their bills by the fifth of the month would receive a discount of twenty-five percent!

Electricity made a huge difference in town and mine. Streets became safer, nights more glowing, schools cheerier, businesses brighter, and home life more comfortable. Along with the telephone, phonograph, automobile, "aeroplane," and motion picture, it seemed that the pace of life could not have quickened or changed more. Modern America had arrived in Silverton.

Culture was being refined as well. No longer would locals patronize a play just because the company had managed to reach their community. The Silverton Standard (January 24, 1903), for example, remarked that "The Drummer Boy of the Rappahannock has come and gone, but leaves no aching void": the play "was a decided disappointment."

When Andrew Carnegie donated money ($10,000) in 1905 for the Silverton Library, the residents constructed a building on Reese Street. There it still stands today, almost as they built it, a time warp through which to enter the past. Not remiss, City Council passed another ordinance including fines for overdue books and annual appropriation of $1,250 a year for maintaining the library.

Andrew Carnegie donated the money for the library on Reese St. Built in 1906, it remains almost a time warp of the day it opened.   *(Courtesy: Glen Crandall)*

A new town hall graced Greene Street by 1909, joining the impressive San Juan County Court House (1907) which showed the permanence and prestige of the now nearly forty-year-old community. Those years-ago founders would have been proud, no doubt, of how their "baby" had grown.

In 1902, the Council got around to ordering the numbering of houses and businesses. All numbers were to be at least three inches high and "placed near main or front entrance." That progressive step aided visitors and residents alike.

Some things change, others stay the same. In 1907, the council hired six extra police officers for Halloween. Despite concern over expenses, the town budgets continued to grow. In 1910, for example, expenditures were $59,059, including $16,000 for the new city hall. Much to locals relief, that was two thousand less than 1907. One major source of revenue remained saloon licenses, totaling $16,000 in 1907. No better weather vane existed as to Silverton's prosperity than this amount. The business district, too, had matured on Greene

Street, with the Red Light District still next door on Blair Street.

Tourism already played an increasingly important role in Silverton and the San Juans. Old-timer Otto Mears in 1902, answered an inquiry about Silverton as a summer resort. While no "so-called summer resorts" were near the town, it has a delightful summer climate. The scenery near and around "here are grand and cannot be surpassed anywhere in Colorado." Then he echoed a refrain that rang throughout much of the twentieth century, "unfortunately however the locality is little known." Others fretted that the region was neglected because of its long distance from "Denver and other central points."

Silverton's Commercial Club made a special effort to overcome these impressions. It organized a special publicity committee, which sent out articles to leading newspapers, "so written as to advertise the resources of the county." It also toyed with the idea of creating a lantern slide presentation and inviting newspapermen to come to Silverton to "show them a time." In 1913 the club published pamphlets, supported good roads, tried to get a railroad into the San Juans from the south (to break the D&RG monopoly), and conducted a letter-writing campaign in praise of San Juan County. By then, the club offered rooms where "social features" proved a great success, affording businessmen "much needed relaxation."

Tourists were welcomed, but eastern Europeans faced a little discrimination occasionally and the Chinese a great deal on several occasions. In 1901-02, Silverton, Telluride, and Ouray forced the Chinese out by boycotting their businesses. The union partly promoted this in their desire for American laborers only; some businessmen, likewise, encouraged their removal to eliminate competition. Brief international tension flared when the Chinese minister in Washington protested to the American Secretary of State. He, in turn, notified the governor, who squelched the matter by reporting there was nothing that could be done, because nothing illegal had been perpetrated on the Chinese.

When a few returned to Silverton, trouble flared anew. In May 1902, a Chinese restaurant and laundry were looted and the

70

owners driven out of Silverton. An appeal was made to the marshal for protection, and the police made an "effort to apprehend" the guilty parties. Fearing more damage to the town's reputation, a "law and order league" was organized to stop the abuse of the Chinese. Silverton was not alone; the United States was going through another one of its periodic "yellow peril" scares.

Silverton had matured into a stabilized mining town by the time of the outbreak of World War I in Europe in 1914. It had even taken on a romantic glow in the memories of children who grew up there during those years. Thomas Bawden recalled that, during one of the times that snowslides cut Silverton off from rail service, he and a buddy made a "small fortune." They pulled their toboggan to the slide sight and picked up some Sunday papers from the train. Hauling them back to town, they found a ready market for as high as $1 a copy. He also fondly remembered the rock drilling contests, especially seeing a "world champion drilling team. They used to

The Silver Lake mine, one of Silverton's most famous and productive.
(Courtesy: San Jaun County Historical Society)

71

call them the world champions. Maybe they stretched the truth on that a bit, but they would have been mighty hard to beat. They called them the 'Terrible Swedes'."

The last glow of this prosperous mining era, the single and double jack drilling contests were a reminder of years gone by. Machines generally did the work in all but the small mines. The times were changing: indications appeared everywhere. Silverton folks could see them no more clearly than in their local newspapers, as they followed events in war torn Europe. Many took sides, despite President Woodrow Wilson admonishing his country to be neutral. War has a way of booming a mining economy, and these years would be no exception. Despite high expectations and optimism, neither the town nor its mines would ever in the decades ahead see such general prosperity again.

CHAPTER 10
"THE GRIM REAPER"

NUMBER OF DEATHS TO DATE TOTALS UP TO 128

MANY OF SILVERTON'S PROMINENT CITIZENS ARE CALLED BY THE GRIM REAPER—

PAST WEEK HAS BEEN THE BLACKEST EVER KNOWN IN THE HISTORY OF THIS DISTRICT

Those headlines from the Silverton Weekly Miner, November 1, 1918, marked the end of a defining moment for Silverton and its people. They had nothing to do with a war, although a war had just ended.

The United States entered World War I in April 1917. By that time, most Americans were convinced that they were fighting to "make the world safe for democracy" and to save it from the barbaric Hun. British propaganda and Americans' natural inclinations had aligned the country on the side of the allied powers. On the other side fought primarily Germany and the Austrian-Hungarian empire.

In 1916, this Buick 6 Touring car was the first to be driven from Eureka to Animas Forks.
(Courtesy: Author)

World War I was in full swing as this parade rolled through Silverton in 1918.
(Courtesy: Center of Southwest Studies)

For the recent arrivals from eastern Europe, the choice was not that simple. They had relatives and former friends fighting on that other side. The war did not split the community, but, here as elsewhere in the United States, patriotism carried the day. If one sympathized at all with the central powers, one had best keep those opinions to himself or herself.

From the American perspective, the war did not last that long, ending on November 11, 1918. Even in those few months, young Silverton men volunteered, boarded the D&RG train, and rode off to war. Stay-at-home Silvertonians purchased war bonds, gathered materials for the war effort, and closely followed developments in the newspaper accounts. For the miners who stayed home, these were good years, especially for the base metal mines.

The war's impact on the community proved small, however, compared with what happened at its conclusion—the great flu epidemic of 1918-19. The twentieth century's greatest scourge, with its complications (particularly pneumonia), killed a shocking 7,783

Coloradans in ten months, and estimates of deaths throughout the world start at twenty-one million people. Known as the "Spanish influenza," this virulent strain of a flu virus proved especially deadly at higher elevations.

Silverton gained a notoriety that it did not want—a higher percentage of people died during the epidemic than in any other town in the United States. While the exact number will never be known, approximately 150 people perished, nearly ten percent of the town's population. In mid-October, at the epidemic's peak, the Silverton Weekly Miner listed forty-two dead the previous week. "In all its history the San Juan has never experienced such a siege of illness and death." San Juan Country residents, before the sickness ran its course, suffered 883 flu and 415 pneumonia cases—a rate twelve times the state's norm.

No matter what precautions people tried they did no good. Schools were closed, public meetings banned, quarantines attempted, masks worn, patent medicine drunk, pills swallowed, and a variety of home cures tried. Colorado had adopted prohibition in 1916, which made the old medical standby, alcohol, hard to come by. Nothing worked, no known cure existed. It "scared you to death, you ached all over," recalled one person. People just died. The plague overwhelmed nurses, doctors, and hospitals.

> Spaces and time will not permit us to give but very little notice of the many sad deaths that have occurred in this community since our last issue. There has scarcely been a household that has not been touched by sickness or death of a loved one or a friend.
>
> (Silverton Weekly Miner, November 1, 1918)

This was surrounded by three quarter page columns of names of those who had died.

Statistics are fine, but what did it mean to the average person? Bessie Finegan, a Durango nurse during the epidemic, remembered it clearly.

> The whole town was in mourning. Everything was shut down. Everybody on the street wore white surgical masks. I don't think it helped much, because everybody seemed to get the flu anyhow. All the nurses

got it.
The nurses were one of the first ones that got it. We were all in bed. We
were really sick. But most of us got better, there were two of us that
died. Doctors got it. It was awful. I was sicker than the rest, I couldn't
walk I was so weak.
Two things happened to you. Suddenly you couldn't breathe, your lungs
seemed to collapse or else you hemorrhaged, and you hemorrhaged...and
you died in a few minutes.

She remembered one story from Silverton that illustrated how fast
this happened. "I remember one time somebody died, and they sent
for the undertaker. And he didn't answer his phone. Finally, they
sent someone to see why in the world he wasn't coming. When they
went in, there were about a half dozen bodies lying there, and he was
lying among them, dead. And that was just how quick he died."

Edna Goodman's family was in the undertaking business. The
victims came so fast that they could not handle them; they just "put a
tag on the toe of each victim." She said it was bad in Durango "but
worse up at Silverton. The miners up there died like flies. They tied
tags on big toes up there too." Her husband went to Silverton to help
but had too much to do at home and came back. Her very vivid
recollection came from her home across the street from the undertaking house. "I could see the death wagon in the morning when I got
up, also in the evening when I went to bed. It was very depressing,
the first thing you saw in the morning and the last thing at night."
She, her husband, and two babies all came down with the flu but
survived. Mary Swanson's widowed mother and older brother died
during the epidemic, leaving her to rear her three small brothers. She
remembered that, among the miners who boarded with her mother,
"the husky and young ones died, the older ones didn't die like that."
That younger people died so frequently amazed people. "Nobody
seemed to know why, they just did." They turned the city hall into a
hospital when the regular hospital was overwhelmed with patients.
Finally, before Christmas the severe crisis passed, the quarantine was
lifted, and Silverton tried to celebrate the holidays.

One small girl's most vivid memory of these tragic months
was seeing wagons stacked with bodies heading for the cemetery.

They buried many of the victims in a mass grave in the Silverton Hillside Cemetery. Then the catastrophe receded in history, and winter turned into spring. Silverton would never be the same again. An era ended with the Spanish Influenza epidemic and World War I— the good, old days receded into memory.

Silverton folk, like Coloradans and Americans in general, pushed the nightmare as far to the back of their minds as they could. They wanted to forget the flu. It was, after all, a "war" they had lost, one that came on the heels of the "war to end all wars." It was, in the words of Macbeth, "Pluck from the memory a rooted sorrow."

Freda Peterson, in her "The Story of Hillside Cemetery," quotes a poem that she credits to a "survivor." The last part catches the tragedy as well as any written account can.

> What is it like, this Spanish flu?
> Ask me brother, for I've been through;
> It is by Misery, out of Despair
> It pulls your teeth and curls your hair,
> It thins your blood and brays your bones,
>   And fills your craw with moans and groans,
>   And sometime maybe, you get well;
>   Some call it flu .... I call it hell!

During 1918 flu epidemic, victims were buried in this mass grave in Hillside Cemetery. (Courtesy: Glen Crandall)

CHAPTER 11

DRYS VS. WETS

"Demon rum" and its cohorts had long raised the ire of re-formers. One reason the liquor interests opposed woman's suffrage, if you recall, was the fear that prohibition would follow. They were right. Colorado became a local option state in 1907, but the prohibitionists fought on, opposed steadfastly by the people concentrated in Denver and most of the mining communities. The battle of the "wets vs. drys" ended in 1914, when Colorado voted dry. On January 1, 1916, Prohibition became the law of the state. For the United States, the eighteenth amendment, in 1920, made the "manufacture, sale, or transportation of intoxicating liquors" (plus importing or exporting of same) illegal. The golden age of national reform loomed at hand. At long last, drunkenness, family abuse, the saloon, and—some optimists hoped—crime and poverty would vanish from the land. That bane of reformers, the saloon, did disappear.

Like many mining and urban areas, Silverton voted wet; however, the drys, especially rural, had carried the day. As explained in an interview by a former resident; "We did not want that dry busi-

Silverton on a wintery November day in 1929. *(Courtesy: Center of Southwest Studies)*

Mining, no matter what era, is hard, dangerous, labor intensive work.
(Courtesy: Durango Herald)

ness. Course, there's been towns like over in Delta, it was dry for years. But the people in Delta used to go to Montrose and drink."

The impact this had on Silverton was instant—on January 1, 1916. One Silvertonian remembered that January midnight, "The saloon keeps started rolling the barrels out in the street. People drinking and raising hell. Course, the law stopped all of that."

The law stopped that, but Prohibition did not accomplish what the reformers expected. In fact, quite the opposite came to pass. Drinking became the socially exciting thing to do, speakeasies replaced saloons, crime increased, along with the cost of enforcing

Prohibition, and bootlegging flourished. Once prosperous mining communities, like Silverton and Leadville, gained new "fame" as bootlegging centers.

What was Silverton like in the heyday of bootlegging, the 1920s? A then Silverton resident, on the promise that he would remain anonymous, recalled those days:

> The stills were in homes, most of them. In the summer time there were some in the hills. A shot cost 25 cents, a quart $2 and a pint $1. There was good, bad whiskey. Some of it would turn up your toenails, I'll tell you that much. Never killed anybody that I know of. Out of here though, I've heard it blinded some people.
>
> See everybody had their brand. Some guy was making better whiskey than the other one. Course they advertised that and that's how it went all the way through.

Like elsewhere, bootlegging had a definite impact on law enforcement and people's respect for the law. After recalling a friend's case of "bribing" a lawyer and judge with ten gallons of fine whiskey, the man continued.

> Pretty soon there was a lot of money in it for the law. So they started collecting from the bootleggers. Lot of the bootleggers, in with the law, could do what they wanted.
>
> Then the federals came in and picked up some of the ones that weren't paying off—most of the time they would put them under bond, then have a big trial in Durango.

There being only one main highway in and out of Silverton, when the "feds" did try a raid, someone would phone ahead a warning from Durango or Ouray. The town seemed "clean," when the agents arrived. When a raid proved successful, Silverton took on a nearly deserted air by the time the accused, witnesses, family, and friends had gone to the trial. Occasionally, wives were arrested along with their bootlegger husbands. A few prisoners were even imprisoned as far away as Pueblo. Not in Silverton, "they didn't keep anybody here that was bootlegging."

One other unexpected side effect surfaced, an increase in drinking by women and children. At least that was the conclusion of one Silvertonian, who said, "They thought they were doing a big thing, they didn't know really how it was to have this Prohibition. They reason, I say, it was rotten, it brought all the youngsters in to drink." The problem got worse.

> Pretty soon the women, kids—everybody got to drinking. But before Prohibition we didn't have this delinquency, children's delinquency, because Silverton would enforce it [law] and the women could not go into the saloons either. Unless, like I told you they had the little wine room.

How open did Silverton become during those days? A woman explained, "You could go in almost anybody's kitchen and buy a drink." People would deliver it in the daytime—and it was safer that way. She told of one raid and her family's reaction.

> Anyway, we had about 700-800 bottles of beer. My father wasn't here or this wouldn't have happened. My sister got real worried. She said 'oh, we gotta get rid of it, get it outta here.' So she got a couple of drunks, mind you, with a car and put the beer in and took it out. Instead

Alvalanches have always been a great danger in the San Juans.
(Courtesy: Silverton Standard and the Miner)

of staying there she come on back to town. When we went out there, they had moved the beer. In the meantime, everybody else is running around hiding their stuff. [The "drunks" had a wonderful party.] My Dad asked them for the bottles. It was so hard to get bottles.

She concluded, "We had different places where we hid it. They never found any whiskey or wine on us though. But boy that beer, I'll never forget it." Almost with a fondness, she recalled, "We always had pretty good whiskey around here."

To the disgust of some, the joy of more, and to the relief of many, Colorado voters repealed statewide prohibition in 1932. The state now permitted the manufacture and sale of intoxicating liquor "to be regulated by statute," except that "saloons should never be permitted." National prohibition ended in 1933; the "great experiment" was over. By then, however, a worse problem affected Silverton, the Great Depression.

Silverton in 1957 waiting for the next boom.   *(Courtesy: U.S. Forest Service)*

A REAL MINING MAN

From the summer of 1925 to early 1953, one man kept Silverton mining alive, Charles Chase. No one individual has ever meant so much to local mining, and nearly as much to the town, as Chase. Silverton native Gerald Swanson paid this tribute to Chase: "During the depression he ran a mine and mill on $4 ore and kept about 150-200 men working, and made it work because he was a real mining man." Chase's Shenandoah-Dives operation became a model of mining in the changing world of the mid-decades of the twentieth century.

San Juan County mining declined in the 1920s and the crash of 1929, was followed by the devastating depression of the 1930s, which hurt even more. For a mining district, Silverton was getting on in years. Only a few make it past twenty-five years. By 1933, only five mines remained open and three of those for only part of the year; production for the year amounted to $795,000, mostly in gold and silver. Of these mines, the Colorado Bureau of Mines reported that "the Shenandoah-Dives mines led all others in the number of men (approximately 250) employed, and maintained an ore production of 600 tons daily throughout the year."

Chase had been manager of Telluride's Liberty Bell Gold Mine, before he came to Silverton with a reputation of being willing to try "many fresh approaches" and able to work a mine profitably with low grade ore. With a college degree in philosophy, Chase was an unusual mining man.

It was said of Chase that no out-of-work, hungry miner who reached his boarding house had to leave hungry. Mary Swanson fondly recalled, "A lot of men used to walk up there every day to get a free meal. Some of them were so hungry, they would walk up to the mine. He fed them all that went up there. He fed a lot of people. He was good to the people." Mining jobs at the mine and mill, however, proved hard to come by, miners did not "tramp down the hill," as they had in earlier days throughout the West. There simply remained no places to tramp to with much hope of finding work.

Even Chase had to ask his men to take voluntarily a reduction in wages of twenty-five percent. He went so far as to ask local merchants and landlords to reduce prices. Only by working together could the mine and town survive. It worked.

General manager of the Shenandoah-Dives Mine and the Mayflower Mill (he built it in 1929), Chase used innovative techniques and bulldog tenacity to keep mining alive. He faced rising costs and lower grade ore during the 1930s depression, a labor strike, World War II shortages, and declining base metal prices after the war and kept mining; nothing stopped Chase and his mining.

Chase and other miners were helped by President Franklin Roosevelt's New Deal program, particularly when it raised the price of gold from $20 to $35 an ounce. By 1939, for instance, twenty-five mines operated with an annual production of $1.2 million. Actually, this represented a sharp decline from the two million plus of

By Chase's era, trucks had become a part of mining. He actually took this photo.
(Courtesy: Center of Southwest Studies)

Trams like this one at the Mayflower Mill, once crisscrossed Silverton's mining district. (Courtesy: Robert Trennert)

1938, reflecting a seven week strike at the Shenandoah-Dives.

Chase, meanwhile, had upgraded his operation and continued development and exploration work throughout his Shenandoah-Dives days. "Foolproof" electrical equipment, "radio address system," new hoists, modern equipment, cost efficient milling and mining—Chase transformed and modernized these, and kept his mine profitably in operation. Said the Bureau of Mines in its 1939 report, discussing Chase's work for the year, it "is up-to-date in every detail."

He also displayed something unusual for mining men during his generation, an environmental awareness. Downstream pollution typically marked the presence of mining and milling. Downstream people and towns did not show much concern; after all, mining eco-

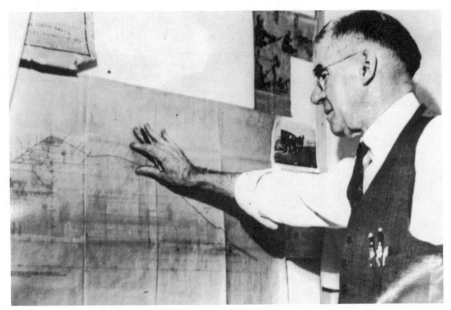

Charles Chase, the man who kept Silverton a mining town into the 1950s.
(Courtesy: San Juan County Historical Society)

nomically aided them. As Chase wrote, when he completed redoing the mill in 1929 that included a settling tank, "at that time every mill in the San Juan region discharged tailings into the nearest available stream. ...and this with little or no protest from people down stream."

Despite his efforts, farmers found their water polluted. In 1935, Animas valley farmers protested. Chase responded at once and underlined this part of a letter to a stockholder: "with firm undertaking to withhold tailings from the stream." Financial strains of the 1930s kept him from completely reaching his goal but he did the best he could, "at a cost within our research." Chase did devise a system of workable tailings ponds.

After the war, however, the situation turned grim again. The dirty-gray, "greenish" colored river distressed farmers, Durangoans, and visitors. Chase wrote, "I am embarrassed that our retention is on a level lower than before. I am distressed." He worked to correct the problems but bristled in an October 1949 letter to the criticizing Colorado Game and Fish Commission, "This company alone, of mine operators in the valley, in conference with down stream farmers, undertook in 1935 to retain its tailing. To date expenditure on the project has aggregated $200,083, $18,053 within this calendar year. This money was not spent as an idle gesture."

Like many mining men since, Chase found himself in a no-win environmental situation. Chase protested that he was not the only mine operating, just the largest. Then came the question, what to do with the no longer operating mines and mills? Each of them potentially contributed their share. Who would pay? Many owners had died and the companies no longer existed, but that did not stop the pollution.

Chase continued this "profitless controversy" until he retired. He even received a commending letter from Durango in September 1952, complementing him on the "the way he is keeping the river clean this summer." Chase proudly replied, "I share with you your satisfaction, having always believed it wrong that the stream should be fouled."

The Mayflower Mill that Chase used to keep mining alive for a generation. It is now a Museum. *(Courtesy: Robert Trennert)*

By 1952, the Shenandoah-Dives had reached the end—ore values continued declining and the gold was gone. When base metals prices collapsed, the mine, marginal in the best of times, began to lose money steadily. The company, too, had changed stockholders. People were now more interested in speculation and stock manipulation than mining and Silverton's present and future, all of which had concerned Chase throughout his career. Faced with a collapsed stock price and rising labor and material cost, company directors voted to close the mine in February 1953. Chase fought to keep it open then and tried the remaining three years of his life to reopen it, to no avail.

Charles Chase faced all the problems that finally ended Silverton's mining era—rising costs, environmental concerns, dwindling ore reserves and lower grade ore, and a declining base metal prices. For keeping mining alive for the decades he did, Chase deserves, as was said in his youth, "Three cheers and a tiger." His enlightened attitude toward mining's environmental responsibilities put to shame many of his contemporaries. A rumor that refuses to die accuses some other Silverton mining companies of having dumped their tailings into the river at night, so that the discoloration would slip past the community and be safely downstream by morning, when the inspectors would be making their examination.

No man was more important to Silverton mining in the twentieth century than Charles Chase. Mary Swanson and others appreciated that, "He was the one who kept Silverton going during the depression." Charles Chase was a mining man's man.

CHAPTER 13

THE PAST MEETS THE FUTURE

December 7, 1941, "a date that will live in infamy," brought Silverton and the rest of the country into World War II. The "treacherous attack" on Pearl Harbor stunned Silvertonians, as it did everyone else. Quickly the town and county went to war. As President Roosevelt said two months later, "Never before have we had so little time in which to do so much." For Colorado and the San Juans, the war years were a watershed.

One more time mining boomed, and Silverton thrived. The war would affect everybody in town. Within days, the mayor and council offered 100 per cent cooperation with Colorado and Washington during this "national emergency." Local folks were alerted to prevent "sabotage" to dams, bridges, "defense industries," and utilities within the city and county. They also read in the first issue of the

Santa Claus is a popular attraction in Silverton regardless of the year.
Courtesy: Silverton Standard and the Miner

Standard Miner, after the attack, that a former Silverton man was killed at Pearl Harbor and that several "Silverton boys in service were in the Philippines and Hawaiian islands." The total war, homefront and warfront, had quickly been brought home to them.

One unexpected December result brought a cheery, encouraging note from the editor: "In the face of this wartime emergency, people should not let themselves be unduly alarmed." The purchase of Christmas goods had taken a sharp drop in Silverton in the days after Pearl Harbor. This Christmas should be more a "day of cheer than ever before. People should continue their holiday buying."

In the following years, Silverton folk traced the news from all war fronts, from the gloom days of '42 to the successes of 1944-45. They also saw the changes that came at home. Additional police were deputized and a six-man committee appointed "to take care of any unusual problems" that might arise. Locals were told to "report all anti-American or subversive activities to the police." By December 19, 1941, the Boy Scouts were already collecting waste paper for the war effort.

Everything that could be done was accomplished to help the war effort. Proceeds from a "patriotic dance" in early June 1942 would be used to "purchase gifts and cigarettes for selectees [draft]." Buying war bonds and participating in bond drives became the thing to do; that June the county quota hit $1,000. The local Post Office posted addresses of Silverton boys in service, so home folks could keep them informed as to Silverton times.

The editor of the paper did become upset over gas rationing. He strongly opposed the idea since supplies seemed adequate. Again, that century old-distrust of the east crept in, "If civilians in the coastal areas," through political pressure push "us to it, it is purely selfish." Gas rationing and rationing in general came, nevertheless. The Standard Miner, like newspapers everywhere, went patriotically to war. War news, a "girls and boys" in service column, photographs, and cartoons kept readers abreast with developments. The radio, too, allowed everybody to stay attuned to the war.

Air raid "exercises" brought home the wartime situation, even

At one time Silverton had one of the country's highest air strips.
Courtesy: <u>Silverton Standard and the Miner</u>

if no real danger existed. Adults and children took part in patriotic programs, as did some war veterans. Silvertonians, however, had problems raising victory gardens for war effort. They learned to mail Christmas packages early, from September 15-October 15, for men and women overseas. They cheered when "better tire recapping" became possible after May 1944. If they had not realized it before, locals learned how dependent they had become on trucks and automobiles, when tires and gas became rationed.

Women learned to take shopping bags with them when going to the grocery store, because of the "critical shortage" of bags and wrapping paper. As the war situation improved, they enjoyed novel ways to buy bonds. A bond party in December 1944 auctioned goods by buying bonds. With some articles bid as high as a $500 bond, it raised more than $23,000. Times were flush as they had not been for decades.

Ration books, draft cards, Red Cross volunteering, and scrap drives became the features of the day. The yearly quotas of the iron scrap drive were easy enough to fulfill, from abandoned mines throughout the county; much of mining's material heritage disappeared in a patriotic frenzy. What was left would be threatened after the war's end by the popular military invention, the four wheel-drive jeep.

Silverton prospered because mining prospered. The government desperately needed minerals to carry on the war. It encouraged greater production.

Mining changed drastically in World War II. By law, the Federal government limited mining to war needed minerals. Only precious metal mines found themselves unable to get needed materials and equipment. Those went to base metal and coal mines. Government control came to the industry as never before. This became particularly obvious, as Washington searched for uranium ores throughout southwest Colorado and elsewhere in the four corner states. Much of Colorado's mining shut down, but not in San Juan County, however.

The 1943 report of the Colorado Bureau of Mines clearly showed San Juan County's significance. "This county is of great importance to the war effort. Notable in this county are the large veins of both high grade and base metal ores." Production of gold and silver continued, of course, but now copper, lead, zinc, tungsten, and manganese were the needed products. Chase kept his Shenandoah-Dives Mine and mill operating, with "large tonnages" of copper-lead and zinc concentrates shipped. Prospecting also was carried on throughout the county in the search for war related minerals.

Silverton mining had not witnessed this much activity in years—fifteen mines operating in 1943. Its $1.5 million production that year ranked fourth in the state. San Juan mining was doing its part to win the war.

In September 1945, World War II finally came to an end. Red Cross workers were encouraged to turn in the "time since Janu-

A proud family stands on Blair Street with their serviceman son. World War II took many of Silverton's young men and women into defense work or the military. (Courtesy: San Juan County Historical Society)

ary 1, 1940" to earn their "pin and service stripes." The <u>Standard Miner</u> (September 17,1945), amid a photo of a landing party in Japan and servicemen looking at the ruins of Corregidor, where the American made a last stand in 1942, had a full page called "WWII Honor Roll." Photos of the five Silverton men killed were surrounded by the names of all those who served; the list filled the whole page. Their hometown, Silverton, and its mines had not been as prosperous since before World War I. For a fleeting moment, the past had returned. Would prosperity stay?

When veterans came home they found Colorado poised on the threshold of a boom that would last for a generation. Urban growth, skiing, new industries, air transportation, increased year-round tourism, growth in higher education, and prosperous times for Denver and its suburbs would be the hallmarks of the new era. Mining, however, might not enjoy those good days. San Juan County had done all right during the war; other counties never rebounded. It cost too much to reopen mines that had barely been surviving before the war. Isolated from the main stream of Colorado postwar development, Silverton still looked to the past, as the present barged onto the scene all around it.

The newspaper saw nothing but a bright future ahead. The editor forecast, "expect big mine development" throughout the San Juans now that the "war is over." That forecast eerily sounded like one from the 1870s or 1890s.

CHAPTER 14

CHRIST OF THE MOUNTAINS

The great, hoped-for mining boom after the war proved short-lived. With base metals—copper, lead, and zinc—carrying the load, San Juan County enjoyed seven years of two million dollars of annual production. One, 1951, topped three million. Into the early fifties, prospects looked good, then came the bust. Boom and bust had been part of Silverton's mining history since the 1870s.

In fact, when Chase closed down the county's largest producer, Shenandoah-Dives, and closed its mill, March 14, 1953, mining nearly stopped. Mineral production collapsed from $2.8 million in 1952 to $123,000 two years later (lowest level since 1882), before rebounding to the $500,000 range in 1956. Silverton's population slipped from 1,375 in the 1950 census to 890 by 1957. Statistics of all types reflected the decline, except the number of old age pension-

In the early 1950s, Silverton, and the surrounding region, provided the location for several movies including Naked Spur starring James Stewart. (Courtesy: Silverton Standard and the Miner)

ers.

Fortunately for Silverton, tourism started to pick up some of the slack. As the Colorado Year Book 1956-58 noted, Silverton now was the only town in the county. "Its atmosphere is reminiscent of old pioneer mining days and many tourists visit it annually." San Juan County, "formerly one of the great [mineral] producing counties in Colorado," offered "many tourist attractions," including "wondrous scenery and a number of ghost towns." Those "ghost towns" all had once been Silverton's rivals.

Tourists drove over the newly improved Highway 550, the only highway in the state with three 10,000 foot passes in a fifty-mile span. Some flatlanders thought that was a bit much, but, once they drove into Baker's Park, they had to drive out north or south. There was no other escape! The completion and modernization of that highway changed Silverton forever.

For a while, Silverton was in danger of losing its passenger railroad traffic. Freight and passenger numbers had declined signifi-

Christmas in the mountains features a tree and plenty of snow.
(Courtesy: Silverton Standard and the Miner)

96

Miners coming off shift at the Sunnyside Mine.
(Courtesy: Silverton Standard and the Miner)

cantly with the completion of the highway, Americans' growing love affair with cars, and the decline of mining. Fortunately, about this time, people discovered the thrill of riding the narrow gauge line between Durango and Silverton, a "trip into yesteryear." While the Denver & Rio Grande repeatedly said it was not in the "entertainment business," a determined group of people in San Juan and La Plata counties thought that trip offered a splendid tourist opportunity. They fought a hard fight to save the line and convinced the railroad to continue passenger travel.

Interest in the narrow gauge line picked up slowly but, by the mid-sixties, had become an important tourist revenue source for Silverton. That development, however, changed everything. The town prospered in the summer time, yet the rest of the year it relied on mining to keep the wolf from the door.

Mining made a slight rebound, then another decline set in; it looked like local mining might finally come to a close. Few prospected the mountains now, and rusting hulks stood where once mines had prospered. Times called for something near a miracle.

It happened. In January 1958, the Catholic Men's Club devised the idea of a shrine. After selecting a site on Anvil Mountain, overlooking the town, they raised funds and donated their time and talent. Within a year, the statue of Jesus, carved from carrara marble in Italy, was "guarding and protecting the town."

Interestingly, shortly after that, Standard Uranium, later Standard Metals, arrived, drove the American Tunnel, and reopened the Sunnyside Mine. Mining was back! Silverton continued onward as a mining town. It seemingly led a charmed life, refusing to die.

The Sunnyside had been one of Silverton's and Colorado's great gold producers back in the heyday of mining. Originally discovered in 1873, the mine had been purchased and brought into prominence by Judge John Terry, a noted milling man. He consolidated a group of claims into one property, built a mill next to Eureka down in the valley, and prospered. After his death, Terry's sons, William and Joe, sold the mine in 1917, and it finally closed in 1930 during the depression.

Standard Metals got the Sunnyside back into operation but had corporation difficulties, including bankruptcy, in 1971, after which operations resumed in full. Vigorously enforced environmental laws gave general manager Allan Bird and his staff problems that the old-timers had never faced. In June 1974, for example, snow runoff washed 100,000 tons of "grey slime" into the Animas River. Hearings, studies, a shut-down until repairs could be made, and a fine resulted. Mining resumed, and the Sunnyside again became the major gold producer in Colorado.

In June 1978, however, the mine suffered a setback from which it never completely recovered. Miners were working in a profitable gold stope under Lake Emma, where the original mine had been found. On June 4, 1978, the lake broke into the workings, emptying thousands of gallons of water and more than a million tons of mud into the mine. It was "one of the most dramatic mining catas-

The train is hauling tourists now, not freight for the mines.
(Courtesy: Silverton Standard and the Miner)

trophes in the history of the San Juan Mountains." Fortunately, it happened on a Sunday afternoon when the crews were at home or it might have killed everybody. The destruction of the Sunnyside's workings proved nearly complete. It took two years of hard, dangerous labor to clean up the mess and reopen the mine. Some areas of the mine, no longer needed, were never cleaned out.

Because of other bad investments, the company again went into bankruptcy, and in March 1985 the Sunnyside closed again. Several mining companies showed interest in the old mine, but the property was finally sold to Echo Bay Mines in November of that year.

Once again, Silverton lived on hope, the hope that Echo Bay, noted for its ability to mine at very low costs, would revive the industry that gave Silverton its birth. The words of that sage, Ben Franklin, however, could be heard quietly echoing down the canyons, "He that lives upon hope will die fasting."

Revival of mining did not translate into year-round prosperity for Silverton. Miners lived in Montrose and Durango, with their larger business districts and other amenities, and car-pooled to their work. Silverton now relied more on summer tourism to get it through the year than on mining.

For a brief time in the late 1940s and early 1950s, Silverton basked in the glory of the movies. The mountain scenery, the train, and the buildings remaining from an earlier era provided the perfect setting for western movies. Hollywood came to Durango and Silverton. They even redid Blair Street to suit their idea of what a "real" western town should look like! The comedy, "Ticket to Tomahawk," started in Durango and ended in Silverton and featured Blair Street and the railroad. "Across the Wide Missouri" starred the San Juan Mountains and Clark Gable. "Naked Spur's" dramatic ending saw villain and hero fight it out on a tram, an unusual use for old-time mining equipment. The "Denver & Rio Grande" displayed the railroad and its history in a colorful, if not always accurate, rendition. In the end, however, Hollywood came and left for a variety of reasons—high costs, the D&RG's reluctance to be an entertainment stage, and changing needs of the movie makers.

More and more, Silverton banked on the train for its livelihood. As the sixties wound into the seventies, passenger numbers steadily increased. The D&RG, despite grumblings, did go into the entertainment business. It had to; declining freight and passenger revenue on the line from Alamosa to Durango to Silverton had forced it to close all but the segment from Durango to Silverton and one from Antonito to Chama, New Mexico. The rails were pulled out and, by the 1970s, all that remained was the "train into yesterday" and its counterpart, Cumbres and Toltec Railroad. It, too, became a tourist attraction but never as popular as the Durango/Silverton line.

Silverton adapted to the changing times by reverting to its heritage and relying on its fascinating nineteenth-century history and architecture. At least, this was the way some of its residents and a host of tourists assumed it should have been. Hollywood's and

100

Christ of the Mountains Shrine has watched over Silverton for forty years.
(Courtesy: Glen Crandall)

fiction's western image captured what people thought Silverton should portray. Gun fights were staged on Blair Street when the train arrived, "decontaminated" Red Light attractions emphasized, honky-tonk piano greeted the arrivals, and "true to life" western souvenirs were available in almost every shop in town. Even "ore" samples were sold on the streets by enterprising youngsters.

Going commercial and emphasizing the legendary "gunsmoke and gallop" West might have pleased some people, but begged the question. That the train, the town, and the mines and mills offered the most authentic vestiges of yesterday did not seem to matter. To some it did, however, they fought to preserve this fast disappearing legacy.

They fought to preserve it, because it was physically disappearing, as four-wheel drive vehicles allowed visitors and others to reach sites previously inaccessible to cars. Visitors carried off their own "souvenirs." That, combined with the ravages of San Juan winters, was turning old mines and camp sites into "ghost" sites, with only a few pieces of evidence remaining to prove that once people had lived, loved, and worked there.

Former mayor Gerald Swanson saw all these changes. Looking back over the years from the vantage point of 1986, he observed, " I think Silverton has digressed as a town since 1945." Where once there had been grocery, clothing, and hardware stores, "today Silverton has become nothing but a gift shop town. All you've got in this town is tourist oriented gift shops and restaurants. You have about 100 days to make it." Store owners came and shops opened with the coming of tourists; they all left together at the end of the season. "All they have to do is put a tombstone at the end of town and say we bury this town until the first of May."

Silverton's permanent residents had to go elsewhere to shop. "If we don't provide these services you have to go out of town and you take what other shopping is left in town out of town." Nor did Swanson feel in the mid-eighties that it would change. "Good roads brought this about. It'll never change." Being optimistic did seem hard. "If mining explodes and we have 500 miners working in this county, it is not going to change the town."

Silverton was still alive, so hope existed. It had not died yet, but again it faced a turning point in its history.

CHAPTER 15
"THE MINING TOWN THAT NEVER QUIT"

By the late 1980s, Silverton had become a tourist-oriented community. It sold itself as one and emphasized the "quality of its early days as a booming, pioneer mining town." This occurred entirely in the summer months, when the Durango to Silverton train ran, jeeping was excellent, and tourists arrived in large numbers. One change came about. The D&RG had sold its Silverton line to Charles Bradshaw, who increased operations and promoted the line extensively throughout the country.

Silverton benefited, but primarily during the summer and early fall months. When snow finally covered the narrow canyon, slides threatened anytime just as they had a century before. The difference was that now no reason existed to keep the tracks open year-round. Jeeping stopped when winter storms arrived, and tourists had, by then, long ago searched out warmer climes.

The community, however, broadened its appeal by sponsoring other activities. The Silverton Brass Band Festival grew to become one of the best in the country. Participants and audience enjoyed a weekend in mid-August(afternoon and evening concerts) under the tent in the park, savoring the music of yesteryear. Hardrocker Holidays was a throw-back to an earlier mining era, with various mining contests to show visitors the skills and techniques of the industry. A folk music festival added another event and weekend's entertainment. They all brought in people and money, but still left the town with the winter and early spring months clear of any major attraction to lure more people.

Skiing offered a possibility; in fact, for a brief while, Silverton held speed skiing races, but the town lacked a nearby airport or easy winter transportation. When Purgatory opened south down highway 550, and Telluride to the west, Silverton's hopes went glimmering. Locals could enjoy the snow—cross-country skiing or even some down hill— and they would have it almost to themselves.

"The mining town that refused to quit" had a population of

Mining might not be what it was in yester year, but Silverton honors it's past with it's Hard Rock Days celebration. Contestants drill in the single-jack contest. (Courtesy: Silverton Standard and the Miner)

716 in 1990; it had not quit, but it was shrinking in population, particularly during the winter months. The Historical Society worked hard to preserve the town's heritage and were able to raise enough funds to build a state-of-the-art archive next to their old jail museum. Silverton was fortunate to have such dedicated, interested people, especially when a fire gutted the 1908 City Hall. With the help of state gaming funds, it was rebuilt in 1994-96. Any visitor to Silverton should take the time to visit the museum, city hall, and county court house to capture a sense of an earlier place and time.

Not all of that earlier place and time could be savored any more in operation. Echo Bay (Sunnyside Gold Corporation) and leasers were unable to keep the Sunnyside Mine in operation. The mine operated for another six years, finally closing in August 1991. It marked the end of an era that had started back in the 1870s. Silverton, the last of the San Juan mining districts to close, now lived on mining hopes and occasional small operations.

What this meant to the town was losing about 200 jobs and

Bicyclers race the train in the Iron Horse Bicycle Race and many of them arrive long before it does. (Courtesy: Silverton Standard and the Miner)

the largest tax base in the county. The next year, the company announced its reclamation plan for the site (estimated cost—$10.5 million), an ongoing project. The American Tunnel, the main entryway, was plugged, tailing ponds were recontoured, grass seeding and fertilization took place, and other environmental work undertaken. The cost commitment for reclamation did not come cheap. As one publication estimated, "the cost of this ongoing work has probably exceeded all the profits the Sunnyside ever produced in its one hundred years of mining history."

What did this mean to Silverton? Silverton folk knew. "When the Sunnyside mine closed in 1991, this town went into a depression, and I don't mean an economic depression." That depression was easy to understand, "when you realize that most of us living in Silverton have deep roots in the gold mining industry." A spark went out, but the town did not die.

Does this mean the end of Silverton mining? Yes and no. The cost of mining today has soared far beyond what the old-timers could have imagined; the cost of opening a mine is almost prohibitive unless a rich deposit is uncovered. Lower grade ore and deeper underground mining add to the expense. The fact that any underground mine would have to compete with less expensive open-pit mining in northern Nevada and elsewhere in the world for the investor's money does not favor the San Juans. Add to this the environmental laws that regulate what can and what cannot be done in the industry. Even with the price of gold nearly twenty times what it was in the 1880s, Silverton mining faces formidable obstacles and an uphill battle.

Despite such troubles, interest in San Juan mining is neither dying nor dead. Gold or silver fever again can spark excitement just as they did a century ago. That gold, silver, and other minerals still await mining in the San Juans cannot be doubted. It only awaits another day, another time, to start again.

Major mining might be ended, and no longer would tourists driving around the county encounter ore trucks, but the visitor can

For the in-shape runners, Silverton offers the Kendall Mountain Run, one of Colorado's premier mountain runs. *(Courtesy: Silverton Standard and the Miner)*

savor mining. In 1996, the Sunnyside Gold Corporation donated Charles Chase's old Mayflower Mill to the San Juan County Historical Society, along with a grant of $120,000 to help convert the mill into a historical tour site. Tours started that year, and visitors gained an unusual inside look at the milling end of mining.

Add to this a tour of the Old Hundred Mine, and mining could be followed from start to finish. Nowhere else in the country could all the key elements of nineteenth mining be seen in one place—the railroad that made it possible, the mine, the mill, and the town that allowed it to maintain itself—all amid a beautiful mountain setting.

As the twenty-first century and the new millennium approaches, Silverton is alive and well. It has survived the boom and bust cycles that killed many of its contemporaries and has not fallen victim to over commercialization and a gaudy, sentimental sense of Victorianism that has overtaken the Aspens and Tellurides of the world. The flavor of an old mining community can still be felt here; in fact, if somehow the old-timers could come back, they would

Silverton has always enjoyed holidays, a tradition that this July 4 float continues.
(Courtesy: Silverton Standard and the Miner)

Silverton has a long musical heritage. Today the brass band and the famous August festival continue that tradition. *(Courtesy: <u>Silverton Standard and the Miner</u>)*

recognize their old community and probably would not take too long to feel nicely comfortable and at home.

Thomas Hornsby Ferril, the noted Colorado poet, loved the mountains and mining. He wrote a fitting epitaph for Silverton and its mining era in his poem "Ghost Town."

> Here was the glint of blossom rock,
> Here Colorado dug the gold
> For a sealskin vest and a rope of pearl
> And a garter jewel from Amsterdam
> And a house of stone with a jig-saw porch
> Over the hogbacks under the moon
> Out where the prairies are.
>
> Here's where the conifers long ago
> When there were conifers cried to the lovers:
> > *Dig in the earth for gold while you are young!*
> Here's where they cut the conifers and ribbed
> The mines with conifers that sang no more,
> And here they dug the gold and went away.

They went away years ago; they dug for gold while they were young. Now they are no more, and their era disappeared with them.

What about those people, their era? As the ghost of Christmas past said to a startled Scrooge in "A Christmas Carol," "I told you these were only shadows of the things that have been. That they are what they are, do not blame me!" Look around; you will never see these people nor Silverton's high-rolling mining days again. They went away, but they left behind their town and its wonderful heritage. It was no Camelot, nor a gunsmoke, mythical west. Ordinary people were trying to carve a home out of the mountain locked valley and make a living in a mountainous land of long winters, beautiful falls, and short summers. Savor and enjoy.

A BIBLIOGRAPHICAL ESSAY

Having sampled the fascinating history of Silverton and its mines, hopefully you will want to mine deeper. In the past twenty years, Silverton and its history have garnered a great deal of attention. No better place exists to start your search into Silverton's past than Allen Nossaman's superb two volumes, Many More Mountains (Denver: 1989 & 1993), the most comprehensive story of the early history of any mining town in Colorado, or for that matter throughout the Rocky Mountains. Equally as outstanding are the various editions of Freda C. Peterson's The Story of Hillside Cemetery (Oklahoma City). John Marshall and Zeke Zanoni cover the post World War II era in detail, with a personal flavor with comments and photos from Silvertonians, in Mining the Hard Rock (Silverton: 1996).

Silverton has attracted a variety of interest over the years. Mining man Allan Bird's Silverton Gold (Lakewood, Colorado: 1986) is an excellent account of the Sunnyside, both historic and first hand. He followed this volume with two lively accounts Silverton: Then and Now (Lakewood, Colorado: 1990) and Bordellos of Blair Street (Lakewood, Colorado: 1993). An interesting look at the town is found in the Silverton Public Library's International Rhubarb Cookbook (Silverton: c1986) presenting historical glimpses and the winners of the July 4 Rhubarb Contest. If possible, visitors should enjoy one Silverton's old-time July 4 celebrations. Doris B. Osterwald, Cinders & Smoke (Lakewood, Colorado: various editions) takes the visitor along the Durango & Silverton into town; the Colorado Railroad Museum provides another look, Coal, Cinders, & Parlor Cars (Golden: c1991). Duane A. Smith, Guide to Historic Durango & Silverton (Evergreen: Colorado: 1988) provides walking tours. For the general overall view of San Juan mining and Silverton's role in it, see Duane A. Smith Song of the Hammer and Drill (Golden: 1982) and Rob Blair (ed.), <u>The Western San Juan Mountains</u> (Niwot, Colorado, 1996).

For the interested person and serious scholar, the San Juan County Historical Society's museum and neighboring archive building are the places to start. One of Colorado's best and most dedicated historical societies, it has been very active in saving and preserving local history. Add to this the Silverton Library with its microfilm collection of newspapers and the story of Silverton unfolds before your eyes. Savor and learn for the past has much to tell us.

The timeless Silverton (1996), setting in Baker's Park ringed by mountains. The past, present, and future meet in one of Colorado's preeninent mining towns. (Courtesy: Glen Crandall)